THE 1.5 GENERATION

INTERSECTIONS

ASIAN AND PACIFIC AMERICAN
TRANSCULTURAL STUDIES

RUSSELL C. LEONG
GENERAL EDITOR

THE 1.5 GENERATION

Becoming Korean American in Hawai'i

Mary Yu Danico

UNIVERSITY OF HAWAI'I PRESS
HONOLULU

IN ASSOCIATION WITH UCLA
ASIAN AMERICAN STUDIES CENTER
LOS ANGELES

09 08 07 06 05 04   6 5 4 3 2 1

Library of Congress Cataloging-in-Publication Data

Danico, Mary Yu.
    The 1.5 generation : becoming Korean American in Hawaii /
Mary Yu Danico.
        p. cm. — (Intersections)
    Includes bibliographical references and index.
    ISBN 0-8248-2695-7 (paper)
        1. Korean Americans—Hawaii—Ethnic Identity. 2. Korean
    Americans—Hawaii—Cultural assimilation. 3. Korean
    Americans—Hawaii—Social conditions. 4. Hawaii—
    Emigration and immigration. 5. Hawaii—Ethnic relations.
    6. Hawaii—Social conditions. I. Title: One point five genera-
    tion. II. University of California, Los Angeles. Asian American
    Studies Center. III. Title. IV. Intersections (Honolulu, Hawaii)

    DU624.7.K67D36 2004
    305.895'70969—dc21
                                                    2003055275

University of Hawai'i Press books are printed on acid-free
paper and meet the guidelines for permanence and
durability of the Council on Library Resources.

Front cover: Photographs courtesy of Tad Tamura and Mary Yu
Danico

Designed by Publication Services

Printed by Versa Press, Inc.

To my loving partner and greatest supporter, Bryceton Nankil Danico, and my daughters, Kaira and Soleil, who remind me what is really important in life, and to my parents, James and Ann Yu, who have helped shape an independent mind proud of her heritage

CONTENTS

PREFACE

When I began my research in Hawai'i nearly a decade ago, I did not imagine the impact my findings would have on me personally. Having lived most of my life in predominantly middle-upper-class white neighborhoods, I have tried not to think about my race or ethnicity. The remarks I heard from my "friends," neighbors, and strangers constantly reminded me that I was not from America, but I overlooked or denied such sentiments. My parents managed, however, to instill in me a sense of pride in being Korean and encouraged me to share my culture with those who were interested in me. I invited friends over for *omurice*, *kimchee*, *deng jang chi ge*, and other Korean dishes.

In 1994 I had a conversation with Dr. Hagen Koo, a sociology professor at the University of Hawai'i at Mānoa, who got me to question my ethnic identity. He asked a simple and direct question: "Are you an *ilchom ose*, a 1.5 (one point five)?" I had always thought that someone who was born in Korea was 0 generation and was insulted by the idea of being one-and-a-half generation. I went home and called my mom in California and asked her if she knew what an *ilchom ose* was. She quickly informed me that I was a 1.5er (one point fiver), since I immigrated as a child but grew up in the states. This short exchange sparked questions in me that plagued my daily activities in Hawai'i.

Hawai'i is special in that the population of Asian Americans, who are obviously an ethnic minority in the continental United States, here are the visible majority. Unlike the continental United States, where I am constantly reminded of my color, ethnicity, and race, in Hawai'i I felt a sense of belonging that I had never experienced. I felt at home. However, I quickly realized that being from Hawai'i means more than just living in Hawai'i and seeing people like myself; it means embracing the culture and people of Hawai'i, shaped by its history, colonization, and early immigrants. Ironically, being in Hawai'i raised my consciousness of being Asian American, even though people of Asian descent rarely identify themselves as such. It also helped me realize that the sociocultural, political, and historical circumstances of Korean Americans in Hawai'i differ significantly from my own immigration experience.

I began my research by getting to know the Korean community. I looked at it through the eyes of a *Katonk* (a term coined to describe Japanese Americans from the continental United States who had no connection to local culture or people; today it is used loosely to refer to any Asian American who is not from Hawai'i). I wanted to conduct research that would lead to better understanding of the ethnic and generational issues facing Korean Americans in Hawai'i. I feel that I have done this, but in the process of conducting my research I also learned more about myself and my family. The remarks of my respondents reveal that although stereotypes, labels, and discrimination affect Koreans, more damage seems to come from internalizing these beliefs, which ultimately influences 1.5ers' relationships with their parents, the community, and non-Koreans, as well as how they feel about themselves as Koreans in Hawai'i.

I am grateful to the first-generation parents of 1.5ers who opened their homes and themselves to me. Even with confidentiality promised to them, many of the respondents acknowledge the possibility of being recognized by other Korean Americans who may end up reading this study. With Hawai'i being such a small place, chances are greater that they will be recognized than if they had participated in a study in Los Angeles. Although they did not want to air their "dirty laundry" for everyone to see, first-, 1.5, and second-generation Korean Americans felt that the need to foster dialogue and promote understanding was more important than what others may think.

Acknowledgments

When I started preparing this manuscript for publication, I met Sharon Yamamoto, then acquiring editor of University of Hawai'i Press. I instantly connected with her and felt her warmth, strength, intellect, and belief in my work. She gave me my first book contract and in the process, we developed a wonderful friendship. Even after she left the press, we stayed in touch. Anyone who knew Sharon couldn't help but be touched by her. The completion of this book is bittersweet. Sharon passed away in December 2002 after her courageous battle with cancer. I want to dedicate this book in memory of her.

I have been blessed to work with another extraordinary editor, Masako Ikeda. Masako is every writer's dream editor. She is kind, thoughtful, intelligent, critical, and generous with her time. She patiently worked with me for the last two years and helped me see the light at the end of the tunnel. I am truly grateful for her expertise and friendship.

There were days when I didn't think I would ever get this book finished, but friends and colleagues read my work, encouraged me along the way, and kept me going.

I want to thank Alvin So, Jonathan Okamura, and Hagen Koo for their insight, critiques, and suggestions at the inception of this book; Wayne Wooden for his thoughtful and supportive comments; Chris Cameron for his meticulous indexing; Brahim Aoude, who encouraged and cheered me on to finish it, and whose unconditional support means so much; Bob and Agnes Suzuki for their mentoring and inspiration; Brett Stockdill, my dear friend and colleague, who shared my daily struggles and accomplishments; Linda Võ, who was readily available to offer words of wisdom and encouragement, not to mention a good vent and laugh; and finally, my "other" parents, Cynthia and Edward Danico, for always being there for Bryce and me with their love and support.

WHO ARE THE 1.5 GENERATION KOREAN AMERICANS?

The 1.5[1] generation, or *ilchom ose*[2] as it is called in Korean, is a concept that originated in the Korean community to describe immigrant children who are not quite first- or second-generation Korean. It was in the early 1970s that Charles Kim, a reporter for *Koreatown,* the *Korean Times/Hankook Ilbo* English edition, wrote an article describing people like himself, who are neither first nor second generation, as "1.5" generation, or *ilchom ose.* Demographically, of course, the notion of a 1.5 generation is impossible; someone born in Korea is technically considered first generation, and anyone born in the United States is considered second generation. The term *1.5 generation,* however, is significant when it is used in reference to certain sociocultural characteristics and experiences of pre-adult immigrants.[3]

The idea of an in-between generation is common around the world. The Chinese refer to children immigrants as *juk sing.*[4] The Japanese, Chinese, and South Asian groups refer to this group as the "knee-high" generation.[5] The expression *ilchom ose* was first used in the Korean community by first-generation Koreans as well as those in Korea to describe the youth and young adults who immigrated as children. As the generation of 1.5ers progressed, so did the intergenerational and cultural issues. A Korean soap opera titled *Ilchom Ose* that aired in Hawai'i for several months characterized this generation as one that is marginalized, confused, and in conflict with their first-generation parents.

Scholars who study this generation have yet to agree on what constitutes a 1.5er. Broadly, the term *Korean American 1.5 generation* has been used as an informal demographic marker to differentiate immigrant children from their parents (first generation) and from American-born (second generation) Koreans. The Korean 1.5 generation has been generally described as those who are bicultural and bilingual and who immigrated to the United States during their formative years.[6] They are socialized in both Korean and American cultures and consequently express both sets of cultural values and beliefs. Aside from this broad demographic definition, there has been no clear consensus on what it means to belong to the 1.5 generation. For example, bilingualism in this group has been defined in several ways—as referring to Korean American 1.5ers who are (1) fluent in both Korean and English, (2) more fluent in English than Korean, (3) more fluent in Korean than English, or (4) not fluent in either. Portes and Rumbaut describe the four different types of bilingualism as follows. *Fluent bilinguals* know English very well and know a foreign language at least as well. *English-dominant bilinguals* have fluency in English but much weaker knowledge of a foreign language. *Foreign-dominant bilinguals* speak the native ethnic language well but are less fluent in English. Finally, *limited bilinguals* have lost fluency in their native tongue and have yet to acquire a full command of English.[7]

Communication, and especially language, is central to transmitting Korean culture from one generation to the next, for it enables shared understandings between the parents and their 1.5er children. Through maintenance of the Korean language and the learning of English, 1.5ers develop bilingualism, which has become one characteris-

2

tic of this generational group. Furthermore, because the Korean language uses honorific talk and carries cultural significance, the language is connected to culture as well. The family plays a significant role in maintaining and extending Korean culture through the celebration of Korean holidays, the enforcement of filial piety, the cooking and eating of Korean foods, and the transmission of this culture through language. Because language and culture are tied to identity, being bilingual and bicultural shapes the way 1.5ers see and express themselves.

However, the level of bilingualism is contingent on several factors: whether the child immigrant was raised in an ethnic community, the role of the family in sustaining the native language at home, the relationships established with peers, and personal views about other Koreans. To say that all those who immigrated at an age between 6 and 15 are considered 1.5 generation would ignore the fact that those socialized in communities devoid of other Korean-speaking children or adults will most likely become limited in their bilingualism and biculturalism. Some children who immigrated at an early age may actually identify as 1.8 or 1.9, meaning that they don't necessarily feel in between first and second generation, but closer to second generation. However, it becomes increasingly clear that geography or locality plays a large role in how one's ethnic identity is formulated. Just as there are children who immigrate at age 3 who can't speak any Korean, there are others who are more fluent in Korean than English largely because of their immediate surroundings and support system. Thus, there is more to the 1.5 generation than age, but their social, economic, and cultural experiences affect their degree of biculturalism or bilingualism.

Sally, a 31-year-old, immigrated to Hawai'i when she was 3 years old. When speaking to her, one would guess that Sally was either second- or even third-generation local Korean. However, she identifies herself as Korean. She grew up in government-assisted homes with her mother, who spoke only Korean. Most of her immediate neighbors were Korean, she attended a high school where her friends were predominantly Korean and local, and she works in a hotel that is run and owned by Koreans. Although she speaks Konglish[8] with her Korean American friends, at work she speaks primarily Korean. Sally shows how defining the 1.5 generation is complex.

Sonia, a 39-year-old Korean American, immigrated to Oregon at age 12; however, her parents instructed her and her siblings not to speak Korean and to speak only English. Her parents felt that in order to succeed in the dominant white culture, their children had to perfect the English language and never let out that they are immigrants. Consequently, Sonia and her siblings do not speak or understand Korean. She states, "You know, I really feel like I'm just American. Yes, obviously I'm Korean. I mean look at me. But I don't speak Korean, don't eat Korean food, don't date Korean men . . . I'm really just superficially Korean." The pressure in the continental United States to assimilate pushed Sonia and her family to leave their culture behind and to become "American." However, the pressure to be American is not as strong in Hawai'i. The influence of local culture makes adapting to dominant Hawai'i culture easier for many Koreans and other Asian immigrants, although there is still pressure to shed their immigrant status by becoming local.

Won Moo Hurh, one of the first to write about the 1.5 generation, argues that the formative years in attaining functional bilingualism are postadolescence and preadulthood, which he categorizes as between 11 and 16 years of age. He argues that during these years, children immigrants are able to make the transition from Korean to English and have developed ways to cope with the changes. To Hurh one of the key characteristics of the 1.5ers is that they are marginalized and isolated from both the American and Korean cultures due to their role in both cultures. Although there is the potential for identity crisis, there is also the potential of benefiting from the "best of both worlds." The lack of information on the 1.5 generation has much to do with the lack of empirical studies conducted on this group.[9]

The 1.5ers are a heterogeneous group shaped by their experiences and, more specifically, by their gender, class, sexuality, and geography. It is through their own experiences that they construct what it means to be a 1.5er in Hawai'i. The sociocultural experience of gaining an ethnic identity is important to examine.

Characteristics of 1.5 Generation Korean Americans

Korean American 1.5ers have not always claimed 1.5 ethnic identity; as child immigrants, they are technically first-generation Korean Americans much like their parents. However, because of their age at the time of immigration, their experiences vary significantly from those of their parents. During the process of their resocialization in Hawai'i, they concurrently renegotiate and reexpress their ethnic identities to accommodate varying cultures and values.

Thus, it may be argued that age at the time of immigration is not a key factor in typifying the 1.5 generation; rather, what is key are the process, the experience, and the sociocultural environment—specifically, the role of family, education, and community in forming and constructing a 1.5 ethnic identity. Although the minimum age of immigration is not important in defining 1.5ers, they must be foreign born with memories of Korea and an understanding of the culture. The maximum age, however, is significant in characterizing a 1.5er when considering Korean child immigrants who migrated in their teens. Individuals in this group are more likely than the preteen immigrants to have Korean accents, and thus are less likely to "pass" as native speakers of English and less likely to switch between generational boundaries.

Although location and environment play a role in language acquisition, teen immigrants are more likely to have difficulty passing as native born. Thus, the Korean American 1.5 generation is conceptualized here as those who immigrated with their family before 13 years of age, have memories of Korea, and are consciously bicultural. In addition, they are fluent in English and can speak conversational Korean; are able to intermingle Korean, "Korean American," and local[10] ethnic expressions; and have an appreciation for Korean culture.

Three main characteristics shape and construct a 1.5 ethnic identity. First, 1.5ers are conscious of being bicultural; that is, they feel that they can identify with Korean, American, and local cultures and are conscious of their Koreanness, Korean Americanness, and localness in varying situations. The degree of identification is not measured here; many Korean American 1.5ers may feel that they can relate more to the "American" or local culture than the Korean culture, with the measure of identification depending on the age at the time of immigration and how the person is received by both the Korean and dominant cultures. For example, a 1.5er who arrived at age 3 is more likely to adapt to Hawai'i's culture and in return be accepted as part of the local culture, whereas a 1.5er who came to the United States at the age of 13 may try to adapt to local culture but will be perceived as an immigrant because of the Korean accent marking his or her immigrant status. Younger immigrants are more likely to have little to no Korean accent when speaking English; thus it is easier for them to pass as being "American" compared with those who immigrated at a later age, who may carry the audible marker of being a product of ESL (English as a second language).

Geographical location also plays a significant role in the identification process. Some Korean American children may grow up in a predominantly white neighborhood, which limits their interactions with other Koreans or Asian Americans. When Korean Americans live in a neighborhood with predominantly Korean neighbors, they may share a continued sense of Koreanness. The family also plays a critical role. Some families may promote and encourage the maintenance of Korean traditions, language, and culture. Other families may encourage their children to assimilate and become as "American" as possible, which often means not speaking the language, not participating in traditional festivities, and so on.

Korean American 1.5ers possess a second characteristic that makes them different from first- and second-generation Korean Americans. The 1.5ers identify with Western (American and local) and Korean cultures and values to varying degrees; but more important, they are able to switch their generational identities from first, 1.5, and second generation and their ethnic identities depending on who they interact with and the particular situation. That is, they are able to present themselves in varying situations as first, 1.5, or second generation or as Korean American, local, or Korean. Depending on the situation, the individual can "fit in" relatively with different groups, become conscious of the new identity, and concurrently express the conscious identity. In some instances, they may be conscious of even being Korean, but depending on the situational experience, 1.5ers have the option to construct and negotiate the generational boundaries. For example, 1.5ers when with non-Koreans may express themselves as more American, but when with first-generation Koreans may switch to being more Korean. The expressions of being Korean, Korean American, and local are presented through language, body language, cultural etiquette, and so on. The 1.5 generation thus are not really caught in the middle between the first and second generations, as Ryu contends, but are in actuality flowing between generational and ethnic identities in varying situations and contexts.[11]

There are, however, constraints on their ability to traverse generational boundaries. Because Korean American 1.5ers are conversationally bilingual, they are often seen as second generation by first-generation Koreans and, therefore, not really Korean. If 1.5ers interact with first-generation Koreans at a conversational level, they may be able to pass as first-generation Korean; however, if the conversations become formal, the first-generation Koreans are likely to recognize them as 1.5ers. It is, however, easier for 1.5ers to pass as second generation or local to first- and second-generation Koreans and non-Koreans. Because they are fluent in English, it is more difficult to detect whether a 1.5er is an immigrant or second generation. Thus, under some situations, 1.5ers may claim ethnic identity but may not be accepted by first-generation Koreans, but at the same time may benefit from "American/local" privilege.

Consequently, 1.5ers must be bilingual—fluent in English but able to speak conversational Korean. Conversational Korean is necessary for 1.5ers to maintain their language ability, which allows them to converse at home and with other Koreans and Korean Americans, but they may not be literate in Korean. In daily life activities, conversation more than writing is used to communicate and to express oneself. Although some Korean American 1.5ers may be literate in Korean, the key marker is that they are able to communicate verbally with other Koreans and Korean Americans speaking Korean. Granted, the majority of 1.5ers are more fluent in English, largely because this generation received most of their formal education in the United States. It is important to note, however, that there are Korean Americans who, through Korean language schools, Korean courses at college, or summer school programs in Korea, become conversant and literate in Korean. Although 1.5ers may be more fluent in English than Korean, they are able to converse and communicate in Korean.

What is also significant about the Korean 1.5 generation is their ability to "code-switch," that is, to speak in both Korean and English in the same sentence. Some

Korean Americans refer to the language of code switching as "Konglish," a combination or fusion of Korean and English. The practice of code switching occurs primarily when Korean American 1.5ers are with other 1.5ers, but it also occurs to some extent with their parents and siblings.

Although speaking Konglish occurs within the family, it is with other 1.5ers that they express being 1.5. Because of their ability to switch the expression of being Korean to that of being Korean American or local depending on the group, 1.5ers are able to switch from one identity to the other, flowing between culture and generation. For example, when 1.5ers are with first-generation Korean Americans, they revert to honorific talk, bow when meeting an adult, serve tea to the eldest, and show signs of filial piety to their parents. When they are with non-Koreans, they interact in a more egalitarian manner and speak English. However, with other 1.5ers, there is no need to cross cultural or generational lines; they are free to just be 1.5. With other 1.5ers, they identify with the sociocultural experience of growing up in Hawai'i with immigrant parents, they identify with having been an "FOB" ("fresh off the boat") at one time and not understanding English or the local culture, they relate to growing up in a bicultural society, and they exchange their family upbringing without explanation. With other 1.5ers, they experience a collective consciousness and understanding of what it means to be 1.5.

How Are 1.5ers Different from Other Korean Americans?

First-generation Korean Americans are those who came to the United States as adults, having lived their childhood and adolescent years in Korea. Their first language is Korean, and although many of them are bilingual, they feel most comfortable speaking Korean, participating in

Korean American communities, socializing with other first-generation Koreans, and partaking in aspects of Korean culture such as food, rituals, and customs.[12] In many ways, it is easier to eat and be familiar with Korean foods in Hawai'i. Korean barbecue, *kimchee, namul, japche, kalbi,*and *bibimpap* are staples in Hawai'i fast-food restaurants. People who live in Hawai'i eat these Korean foods on a regular basis. However, those who identify as Korean seek out "real" *kimchee* versus the watered-down cabbage, and other Korean foods not commonly found in fast-food establishments.

All this is not to say that first-generation Korean Americans do not socialize with non-Koreans or with 1.5 or second-generation Korean Americans, for many of them do. But first-generation Koreans feel more comfortable with other first-generation Koreans. Furthermore, due to their distinct Korean accent and ties to Korea, first-generation Korean Americans cannot pass as American but are seen by others as immigrants or FOBs. Unlike the 1.5ers and second-generation Korean Americans, most first-generation Korean Americans do not want to pass as anything but first generation. They maintain pride in being Korean and promote social and working relationships with other Korean Americans.

Research on Korean immigrants suggests that they are not assimilable but are able to adapt to various situations.[13] Those who have been studied live primarily in Korean American communities in cities such as New York, Chicago, and Los Angeles.[14] The notion of Koreans as unassimilable has much to do with the fact that they make little attempt to go outside their Korean social network.[15] However, it is important to note that such behavior is largely due to a system that does not welcome or see Asian Americans as "American"; instead they are perpetual foreigners.[16] In acknowledgment of the institutionalized racism, first-generation Korean Americans make no pretense of creating non-Korean ties, but encourage intra-Korean social and economic exchanges in the community.

The second-generation Korean Americans also suffer from institutionalized racism, but because they are born and raised in the United States, they are ascribed American status at birth. Immigrant children and U.S.-born children of immigrants are the fastest-growing segment of the country's total population under 18 years of age. In 1997, they accounted for one out of every five American children. Some 40 percent of the post-1960 immigrants arrived in the United States under the age of 18, and another 40 percent arrived as young adults between the ages of 18 and 34. Only one in ten immigrated after the age of 40. Out of the 28 million persons who make up the second generation, 16 million, or 58 percent, were born between 1960 and 1997.

The 1.5 and second generations clearly constitute one of the fastest-growing groups. Although they are often spoken about as a single group, the two generations are significantly different for several reasons. The second generation, unlike the first and 1.5 generations, inherit all of the basic legal rights of being an "American," including the capacity to run for president of the United States; but more important, they have an inherent sense of Korean American identity. For second-generation Korean Americans, English and American/local culture are primary, and Korean language and culture are secondary. This group is often seen as having generational and cultural clashes with their parents and other first-generationers. Although some second-generation Korean Americans are bilingual and bicultural and may relate to both first- and 1.5 generation issues, they identify and express themselves as American-born Koreans and cannot relate to being an immigrant.

Korean American 1.5ers are distinguishable from the other two generational groups in that they are foreign born yet are able to pass as American born. When 1.5ers immigrate to Hawai'i, they bring with them their

Koreanness. Their experiences in Korea, their memories of life in Korea, their participation in Korean culture, and the social interaction they had with other Koreans influence 1.5ers' basic sense of what it means to be Korean, which is further sustained through the influence of their family. Thus, at the time of immigration the Korean children's sense of identity is Korean. However, the group's sense of ethnic identity transforms with a series of sociocultural experiences and external influences that ultimately contribute to the process of becoming 1.5 Korean American. The young Korean immigrants do not come to Hawai'i with 1.5 ethnic identity. It is through the process of interacting with other Koreans and non-Koreans that they construct their 1.5 ethnic identity.

In Hawai'i, 1.5ers go through a process of resocialization and are exposed to external influences. They come with a sense of Korean identity and then are expected to learn a new set of cultural values and norms. As children of first-generation immigrants, they are continually exposed to Korean influences from their families, and depending on where they live and the community they are exposed to, their connection to being Korean varies. It is within the family, neighborhood, and community that Korean identity is enforced and maintained. The parents have the power to sustain Koreanness through the practices of speaking Korean, eating Korean food, watching Korean television, reading Korean newspapers, socializing with other Koreans, and so on. If the parents early on do not perpetuate Koreanness to their children in the home, the children will have a difficult time maintaining their Korean ethnic identity.

The family also influences what it means to be Korean American. As the roles of the family members change, parents and children reconstruct what it means to be a family in Hawai'i and consequently learn what it means to be a Korean American family. Thus, the family plays a critical role in the process of becoming 1.5 Korean American. They are the primary contributors to the

Korean side of the 1.5ers' bicultural and bilingual abilities, but they also influence how their children view what it means to be Korean. The passing of family values, customs, and traditions is reinforced by the parents. Although 1.5ers may identify with being Korean at this part of the process, they are not seen as really Korean by their parents and other first-generation Korean Americans. First-generation Koreans view them as being more second generation and, because they are not accepted as really Korean, 1.5ers become alienated from the first generation. Thus, there is the notion of privileging Koreanness in the family. There is a value placed on being "really Korean" within the family.

Although the family affects 1.5ers' understanding of what it means to be Korean in the home and with other Koreans, in the process the 1.5ers also learn how the community, the people of Hawai'i (from now on referred to as the larger society), view Koreans, and thereby learn what it means to be Korean American. The larger society is characterized by media portrayals of Koreans as generally first generation, the sociohistorical presentation of Koreans as bar hostesses or taxi drivers, and local people's impressions of Korean Americans as aggressive and hot-tempered, and as owners and workers in Korean bars. Thus, in the local community and schools, 1.5ers learn how others view Korean Americans and interpret from these stereotypes what it means to be Korean American and local.

By this point, 1.5ers have acquired an understanding of what it means to be Korean and Korean American from their family and have learned stereotypical images of Korean Americans from the larger society. They no longer see themselves as Korean, for their exposure to the larger society has given them a new sense of being Korean American in Hawai'i. However, the impressions set forth by the larger society are not always positive. The larger society's stereotypes of Korean Americans influence the way the 1.5ers view themselves and other Koreans in

Hawai'i. As a result, during this part of the process, 1.5ers feel ashamed and embarrassed of being Korean and begin to distance themselves from their Korean identity. They assert a Korean American or local identity to disassociate from the larger society's image of Koreans in Hawai'i. Even though they may assert a Korean American/local identity, second-generation Korean Americans and the larger society remind them that they are not really local and are more first generation than second. Thus, even with their ability to pass as second generation, they are not fully accepted by other groups and hence remain marginalized from both first- and second-generation Korean Americans.

Although social constraints hinder the 1.5ers' ability to pass as first generation, their experiences provide them with alternative ethnic options as Korean American or local in differing situations. However, during their resocialization their feelings of alienation from first-generation, second-generation, and non-Korean groups reaffirm their feelings of not belonging. It is when 1.5ers encounter other 1.5ers that they have a sense of collective ethnic identity. Their bilingual and bicultural attributes are shared by other 1.5ers, and they feel for the first time as if others understand their feelings of "dementedness." By meeting other 1.5ers who do not fit the stereotypical images put forth by the larger society and who do not act like first-generation Korean Americans, 1.5ers experience other Korean Americans who demystify their stereotypical notion of Koreans. Thus, they find a group of Korean Americans with whom they can be proud to associate and who accept them into their circle. The process of becoming a 1.5er or the discovery of being a 1.5er is actualized when they meet other 1.5ers.

After they embrace a collective 1.5 generation identity, 1.5ers begin to participate in Korean and non-Korean communities to dispel the prevalent stereotypes of Korean Americans in Hawai'i. The 1.5ers become active members of both the Korean and larger communities and begin the process of educating others, both Koreans and non-Koreans, about being Korean Americans in Hawai'i.

The socialization process consists of (1) an understanding of what it means to be Korean and learning what it means to be Korean American; (2) resocialization in Hawai'i and learning what it means to be Korean, Korean American, and local; (3) negotiating the ethnic identities but continuing to feel marginalized; (4) meeting other 1.5ers, gaining pride in being Korean American, and acquiring a sense of collective 1.5 ethnic identity; and for some (5) participating in Korean and larger-society activities to deconstruct the current stereotypes of Korean Americans in Hawai'i. The significant point of the process is that not all of the child immigrants will gain a sense of 1.5 ethnic identity. For example, some 1.5ers who experience the benefits of passing as local or second generation may deny their generational and Korean identity altogether and pass as second-generation Korean American or local rather than deal with the negative images. Furthermore, some 1.5ers may achieve a sense of collective identity but may continue to internalize the shaming stereotypes. Thus the process is not unilinear but bidirectional.

Once Korean Americans self identify as 1.5ers, they express themselves as neither first nor second generation, but as "somewhere in between" or "1.5." They are bicultural and conversationally bilingual and are able to switch their ethnic identities; that is, they are able to change the way they express themselves from "more American" to "more Korean," and for Korean Americans in Hawai'i to "more local."[17] The 1.5ers can identify with Western (American), local, and Korean cultures and values in varying degrees, and in a given situation they can "fit in" and be accepted by other Koreans and non-Koreans. However, what is key are not the characteristics of the 1.5 generation, but the process by which they gain the 1.5 ethnic identity. The process of becoming a 1.5er is critical in examining how and under what conditions

1.5ers acquire and negotiate their unique sociocultural characteristics.

Studying the 1.5 Generation

When I began my research in the winter of 1996, I was optimistic about gaining access to the Korean American community and its members. After all, I am Korean, so how difficult could it be? I quickly realized that the visible Korean community consists of predominantly first-generation Korean Americans who are not open to discussing their lives or their family with a "stranger." Thus, for the first few months, I found myself visiting and observing people in Korean-owned or -patronized establishments such as restaurants, grocery stores, churches, hotels, and bars. Although my days at the various sites helped in my observations of Korean Americans in Hawai'i, it fostered very few case study relationships. It was a humbling experience. I realized what Whyte (1984) and Okamura (1981) meant when they spoke of the difficulties and complexity of getting into a clique or group. Although I did not meet 1.5ers as quickly as I would have liked, the fact that I frequented the various Korean establishments made me visible and often allowed me to listen in on conversations and observe interactions of first-, 1.5, and second-generation Korean Americans in Hawai'i.

I began to use my everyday understanding of Korean Americans to pick them out wherever I went. How does one pick out a Korean American? Are there particular features, mannerisms, and behavioral characteristics that are distinguishable only to Koreans? The answer is yes and no. There are some distinguishable physical traits of Koreans, but such views imply that all Koreans look alike, which is far from the case. However, everyday interactions with Korean Americans make one more aware of Korean gestures, mannerisms, language, and overall presentation of being Korean. Thus, Korean Americans who grew up in predominantly non-Korean communities would have a more difficult time differentiatingthe Koreans from other Asian Americans. My everyday understanding of Koreans is based on my experiences and observations of them in northern California; thus, my commonsense understanding of Koreans had limited applicability to local Koreans. Perhaps my impressions were formed by the various stereotypes I held about Koreans, but distinguishing Koreans from other Asian Americans was challenging The expressions and presentations of Korean 1.5ers in Hawai'i proved to be significantly different due to the influence of local culture. Although first-generation Korean Americans were similar to those in the U.S. mainland on the basis of language, Korean accent, and Korean mannerisms, the 1.5 and second-generation Korean Americans were able to shield their Koreanness by presenting themselves as more local. Hence, picking out the 1.5ers in a group became a challenge. Unless they are with other Korean Americans, it is often difficult to determine (1) whether a person is Korean, (2) which generation they are from, and (3) with which ethnic options they identify. Thus, the process of randomly selecting and meeting 1.5ers off the street was not pragmatic for the type of research I wanted to do.

The main research technique used in ethnography is participant observation and fieldwork. In his discussion of fieldwork, Blumer (1969, p. 38) points out that there is a "persistent tendency of human beings in their collective life to build up separate worlds, marked by an operating milieu of different life situations and conceptions for handling these situations." He concludes that to study group life adequately, the researcher has to know these worlds, and that to know the worlds one has to examine them closely. No theorizing, however ingenious, and no observation of scientific protocol, however meticulous, can substitute for developing a familiarity with what is actually going on in the sphere of life under study. I did not want to be a voyeur researcher who merely visited a community for a few weeks and then drew conclusions from it. I knew that I had much to learn from the local Korean community as well as the first-generation Korean American community.

Consequently, as Blumer suggested, I spent countless days observing, talking to, and engaging with Korean Americans in various settings. I found that once I met one Korean Amerian 1.5er, I was quickly introduced to another, so I used snowball sampling.[18] As one first-generation Korean taxi driver stated, "Koreans are a difficult group to meet. While it is difficult to enter the inner circle of Koreans in Hawai'i, once you are accepted, they treat you like family." I realized that this was very true for the Korean American community in Hawai'i. Snowball sampling provided me with an introduction to various Korean 1.5ers, their family, and their community, and the recommendations of Koreans provided a sense of legitimacy and respectability.

The hours of formal and informal interviews allowed me to address the complexity of ethnic identity formation—specifically, the ways in which 1.5ers negotiate generational and ethnic boundaries, under what circumstances 1.5ers switch among their multiple ethnicities, and the process by which 1.5ers construct their distinct ethnic identity. Furthermore, I was able to follow my respondents for a period of one year, which allowed me to see and interact with them in the community and everyday situations. The qualitative method allowed me the time and flexibility to address the multifaceted dimensions of ethnic identity; the limitation is that with an ethnographic approach, the sample must be small. The need to get fully into the case studies' lives makes it impractical to establish a large sample base. The findings from this research are based predominantly on interviews with fifty Korean American men and women in their middle 20s and early 30s, of whom twenty participated in in-depth interviews and eight allowed me into their lives for over one year. However, I argue that although the number of case study respondents may be small, the complex issues that emerged through the use of this method could not have been addressed through other research methodologies.

There were some obstacles. Given that I identify as a Korean American 1.5er from California, I consistently had to reflect on my personal biases to ensure that my own sociocultural experiences and my own understanding of being a 1.5 generation Korean American did not influence the way I interpreted 1.5ers in Hawai'i. Moreover, because I am not from Hawai'i and had limited time on the island, I had to be cognizant of my "outsider" role and also had to learn more about local culture through field observations. Interestingly, most people, Koreans and non-Koreans alike, assumed that I was local. Such assumptions made it easier for me gain entrance into various Korean and local communities. The year I spent with my research subjects allowed me to really get to know my participants. I saw them interact with their friends, family, co-workers, and local community, which allowed me to see the whole experience as opposed to a fragment of the 1.5ers. Some referred to our interview meetings as therapy and introduced me to their friends as their "shrink." The jokings reveal how much I was able to get to know about my subjects' lives, thoughts, and goals. Several of them told me, "You know me better than many of my friends." The trust and friendship that my subjects gave me allowed me to see the complexity of the child immigrant experience in becoming American and local, maintaining a Korean identity, and accepting an in-between status.

I looked for adult participants in their 20s and 30s who had experienced immigration, had Korean and Korean American influences, and identified with being a 1.5er or a Korean American who is between first and second generations. Thus, the participants selected for this study are in some ways the "ideal" 1.5ers who have gone through the identity development process and can reflect on the influences and their effects on the 1.5 ethnic identity. The 1.5ers in this study have the characteristics described earlier—they are bilingual, bicultural, and able to negotiate generational and ethnic boundaries—but what is significant are their sociocultural experiences and how the process has constructed their sense of being 1.5ers. The participants had to be willing not only to spend countless hours with me, but also to let me into their inner circles, specifically their family and community. With the entrance into the inner circles I could observe how 1.5ers negotiate ethnic and generational boundaries in different situations.

The process of meeting Korean 1.5ers in Hawai'i was initially slow, but I quickly realized how small the island of O'ahu really is. As I met one, I was quickly introduced to another. The fear of respondents not having time to meet with me was unfounded. I did not have to make all the effort; respondents frequently called me to set up meetings and invited me to social and family gatherings.

To examine sociocultural influences on the formation of 1.5 ethnic identity, I conducted informal (2-hour) interviews with fifty participants, twenty of whom agreed to in-depth interviews.[19] I met my respondents at Korean churches, at the University of Hawai'i, at Chaminade University, at Korean community functions, and through other Korean Americans. In addition, I met some of my respondents at coffee shops, parties, beach picnics, and organized meetings. I felt that in order to address the process of becoming a 1.5er, I needed to utilize an ethnographic approach with a smaller number of case studies. Thus, of the twenty in-depth interviewees, eight became case study participants. The 1.5er case studies are Jenny Lee, Travis Chung, Dan Kim, Hilary Kim, Andy Shim, Pat Oh, Sean Chung, and Steve Park.[20]

To examine the identity development process, I separated the case studies on the basis of the various outcomes in the process. I examined the effect of family on Korean and Korean American identity, the influence of the larger society on Korean American and local identity, collective consciousness and identification with being 1.5 generation as affected by meeting other 1.5ers, and efforts to recreate the image of Koreans in Hawai'i through participation with Korean and local communities.

The methodology to investigate the role of the Korean American community was not as easy to design. Although the composition of Koreans in Hawai'i consists of first, 1.5, second, and even third generations, the image of the Korean American "community" involves primarily first-generation Korean Americans and reflects mostly tourism, small businesses, restaurants, bars, churches, voluntary organizations, and retail stores. Thus, to suggest that there is a concrete Korean community is premature. Although the Korean community influences 1.5ers indirectly through parents, stereotypes, and community news, 1.5ers are not actively involved in Korean community affairs. There is only one self-described 1.5 generation Korean organization in Hawai'i: the Korean Junior Chamber of Commerce, from now on referred to as the Korean Jaycees. The Korean Jaycees is composed of first-, 1.5, and second-generation members, but the organization expresses itself as neither first nor second generation focused. The officers state that although there are a small number of first-generation Korean American members, the majority are Korean American 1.5ers. Thus, to examine how 1.5ers actively participate in the community in attempting to dispel Korean American stereotypes, I conducted a case study with the Korean Jaycees. For one year, I attended and interviewed members at their general meetings, philanthropic events, social events, and private parties. Throughout the year I observed the relationships within the organization, specifically along generational lines. I was able to study under different social and organizational situations the way in which 1.5ers negotiated generational and ethnic boundaries. In addition, I was able to observe their interactions and expressions of their ethnicity with local and first-generation Koreans at various community functions.

Throughout the course of one year I spent over 100 hours with the 1.5er case studies. I met with the 1.5ers at restaurants, coffee shops, beaches, their homes, social gatherings, and friends' homes. I met with each respondent approximately twice (8 to 10 hours) a month throughout the course of the year. Consequently, I was able to observe the 1.5ers with their family, friends, and peers, which provided me with the opportunity to speak with their parents, second-generation siblings, extended family members, boyfriends or girlfriends, peers, and family friends. Not only was I able to ask about family, but I was able to observe firsthand the family's social interactions. The 1.5ers' use of Konglish, code switching, and negotiation of ethnic and generational boundaries were observable. Through observations and informal interviews, I was able to abstract how the 1.5ers' experiences and influences are intertwined in the process of developing a Korean American 1.5 consciousness.[21]

With each case study, I asked structured and unstructured questions about their 1.5 identity and observed their words as well as their social relationships with each other. The in-depth interviews provided rich data about the experiences of being a Korean immigrant and being Korean 1.5, and furnished a better understanding of the role of the 1.5ers, community, and family in the construction of Korean American 1.5 identity.

In this book I use the abovementioned methods to interpret and analyze how Korean American child immigrants construct and shape their ethnic identity. Specifically, I argue that the family, community, and socioeconomical and political factors influence how 1.5ers see themselves and how others perceive 1.5ers. In Chapter 2 I provide a background on Koreans in Hawai'i by addressing the history of Korean immigration, the social characteristics of Koreans in Hawai'i, and the current demographics of Koreans in Hawai'i. In addition, I present discussions on what it means to be local in Hawai'i and how that differs from the continental U.S. immigrant experience. In Chapter 3 I discuss various theories on the roles of family, community, and environment in the development of ethnic identity. I discuss how social ecology shapes the perception of self and others; how this perception is based on interactions with the family, community, and larger social issues; and how these theories help explain the identity formation of 1.5 generation Korean Americans. In Chapters 4 and 5 I examine the family's influence in maintaining a Korean identity and creating a Korean American identity. I looked at both working-class and middle-class Korean American families. Although family affects ethnic identity, class helps shape the values, structure, and experiences of families. It is important to note that although the families in this study may not represent the typical working- or middle-class family, they do help to illustrate the influence of family in maintaining and creating Korean and Korean American ethnic identity, and at the same time show the divergent social class views about dating, maintaining identity, and perception of being local. To examine the impact of the community and the larger society on Korean American ethnic identity, I discuss in Chapter 6 the effect that stereotypes have on Koreans and non-Koreans, and how the perceptions and labeling of Korean Americans in Hawai'i affect 1.5ers' sense of being Korean American. The discussion of collective consciousness is also highlighted by the eight case studies. In Chapter 7 I include two case studies of Korean American Chamber of Commerce (Korean Jaycees) members, Sean Chung and Steve Kim, and informal interviews with other Jaycee members to discuss the efforts of 1.5ers to transform the image of Korean Americans in Hawai'i.

What's Unique about Studying the 1.5 Generation?

Studies on immigration have thus far focused primarily on the first-generation adults, neglecting the young children who later become active adult members in their communities. In addition, studies of ethnic identity have been focused either on the native born or immigrants, again ignoring the identity of those who are neither immigrants nor native born. When 1.5 generation issues are addressed, they are often linked to the second-generation label of "post-immigrants,"[22] when in fact the 1.5ers' sociocultural experiences are different from those of the second generation. Thus far, 1.5ers have been invisible in the discussion of identity expression and construction. Although some researchers on Koreans allude to the "1.5," there has yet to emerge systematic research on this "other" group. I propose to address this void in research by empirically studying the 1.5ers in their everyday lives and, at the same time, by gaining a better understanding of the process of identity formation. Moreover, this study will add to the much-needed library on Korean Americans. With most Korean immigrants heading to California and Hawai'i,[23] Hawai'i is an ideal place to conduct this research. Korean Americans in Hawai'i have to negotiate not just two cultures but three. Because there is a strong sense of localness in Hawai'i, the setting provides a unique opportunity to observe and address the external and internal influences that shape 1.5ers' ethnic options. Specifically, under what conditions do Korean Americans express themselves as being first generation, Korean American/local, or 1.5 generation?

Finally, this study will show how the process of ethnic identity development in 1.5ers is distinct. Unlike immigrants who maintain the status of being first generation, the 1.5 generation, although technically first generation, is perceived by the first generation as second generation, is seen as more first generation by the second generation, and is viewed ambiguously or as just Korean by non-Koreans and locals. The Korean 1.5ers share a unique experience in Hawai'i, which ultimately transforms their Korean immigrant identity to one of Korean American 1.5 generation.

The Korean 1.5 generation also is unique in that they have been socialized in both Korea and Hawai'i. As a result of having experienced and understood Korean culture, and learning in their resocialization what it means to be a 1.5er, they are able to switch their identities depending on the situation, relationship, and social circumstances. My research is the first empirical study to address the social process in which Korean child immigrants go from immigrants to 1.5ers. By examining the sociocultural influences, this research inaugurates the Korean American 1.5 generation into the mainstream discussion about identity formation and race relations. Ultimately, this examination of ethnic identity construction among Korean Americans will make a new contribution to studies of ethnic identity construction among other immigrant minority groups, such as Filipinos, Vietnamese, and Southeast Asians, addressing an important dimension of the increasing number of 1.5ers in Hawai'i and the continental United States.

2

KOREAN AMERICANS
IN HAWAI‘I

Asian Americans are one of the fastest-growing ethnic minority groups in the United States.[1] The increasing numbers and diversity of nonwhite immigrants since 1965
have challenged the binary approach that once defined
race relations in the United States. The new wave of immigrants includes people who are still distinguished
racially in the United States but who migrate voluntarily,
often under an immigrant preference system that selects
for people with jobs and a level of education that place
them well above their co-ethnics economically.[2] Studies of
Korean immigrants in the United States have increased in
number in recent years, addressing their history of immigration;[3] their adaptation and assimilation to the United
States;[4] their role in the economy;[5] conflicts with other
ethnic groups, primarily African Americans;[6] and to some
degree the generational differences between first- and
second-generation Koreans.[7] Although there has been a
growing interest in the identity and affiliations of Korean
immigrants, very little research has been conducted on the
ethnic identity of their American-born children, and almost no research exists on the young children, the 1.5
generation, who immigrated with their parents.

The Transformation of the Korean American Community

The year 2003 marks the official 100th anniversary of Korean immigration to Hawai'i; however, it was with the passage of the 1965 immigration act that Hawai'i and the rest of the United States experienced the largest influx of Korean immigrants. What is significant about this wave of Korean immigrants is that this group consisted primarily of women and children who reunited or came with family members.[8] The young child immigrants, referred to as the "1.5 generation," and their first-generation parents are the pioneers of what is known as the Korean American community. This chapter looks at the history of Korean immigration to Hawai'i, describes the social positions of Koreans in Hawai'i based on the 1990 Census,[9] and examines the Korean American business and organization community based on *The Korean Directory of Hawai'i*, 1997.

The purpose of this chapter is twofold: to examine the sociohistorical experiences of Koreans in Hawai'i and to provide a picture of how Korean Americans are situated and presented as a community in Hawai'i. By providing a sketch of Korean Americans in Hawai'i, we can better understand how 1.5ers view themselves as Koreans in Hawai'i and how they differ from the first and second generations. Furthermore, this information can help us understand the sociocultural and economic relationships that define Korean American families, communities, and the 1.5 generation's sense of ethnic identity. Finally, this chapter explores how Koreans living in Hawai'i experience culture, race relations, and ethnic identity differently than Korean Americans living in the continental United States.

History of Korean Immigration to Hawai'i

In his book *Korean Immigration to Hawai'i*, Wayne Patterson documents how missionaries as well as government officials were sent to the United States on a goodwill mission to obtain American advisors and $2 million for Korean modernization. According to the Bureau of Naturalization, the first "Korean" in Hawai'i arrived in 1901.[10] But the first wave of immigrants consisted of exchange students and plantation workers who arrived in Hawai'i in 1903. Due to the political situation of the time and the back-door manner in which various U.S. immigration officers handled Korean laborers, some Korean immigrants registered themselves as Chinese ("paper" Chinese).[11] Approximately 7,900 Koreans arrived in Hawai'i from 1903 to 1905. Ninety percent of them were men, 6 percent children, and 4 percent women.[12] This is the official period when Korean immigrants arrived as free laborers for the sugar plantations. Horace Allen, who had strong political ties with the Korean king, recruited these plantation workers. The primary purpose of recruiting Koreans was to counteract the Japanese plantation workers, who were threatening to strike. Due to the Japanese colonization of Korea, Koreans were an ideal group to use against the Japanese laborers.[13]

The presence of Korean laborers created greater racial diversity among workers. Although the majority of Koreans maintained the sojourner mentality and planned to return to Korea after the Japanese occupation or when they had earned enough savings, most found that the sociopolitical conditions in Korea had not improved sufficiently for them to want to return.[14] The Methodist missionaries also contributed to Korean emigration. American missionaries offered new hope to famine-stricken and economically deprived families of North Korea for a better life in Hawai'i.[15]

At this time, Japanese laborers constituted up to 75 percent of the sugar plantation workers in Hawai'i. Korean plantation workers were unwelcome to the Japanese laborers and to some extent unsuccessful as laborers. While they were seen as diligent and hard working, plantation owners stated that the Koreans were not as efficient as the

Japanese. As the number of Korean workers increased, Japanese laborers asked their government to influence the Korean government to stop Korean emigration. As a result, from 1905 to 1940 there was a decline in Korean laborers but an increase in the number of college students, picture brides, and orphans immigrating to the United States.[16]

30

Following the onset of the Korean War, immigration reports show that between 1952 and 1982 over 40,000 Korean brides came to the United States as spouses of American citizens, with an overwhelming percentage of the women married to servicemen stationed in South Korea.[17] The Immigration Act of 1965 led to a drastic increase in the number of Korean immigrants to the United States. Social and political insecurities in South Korea pushed many Koreans to immigrate to Hawai'i and the mainland in hopes of finding better lives in America.[18]

Post-1965 Korean immigrants are predominantly middle- and upper-middle-class professionals. However, the number of Korean immigrants has been declining since 1988. There are several reasons for this reduced number. First, there was much publicity in South Korea about Korean immigrants' adjustment difficulties in the United States. Second, Koreans have experienced better economic, social, and political conditions since the Seoul Olympics in 1988 and, therefore, have seen little reason to leave their homeland.[19] In the early 1990s, the improved economy in Korea and the media's portrayal of black-Korean conflict during the LA uprisings affected how Koreans and Korean Americans perceived the social and political climate in the United States relative to Korea. Consequently, the number of professional immigrants has drastically decreased and recent immigrants have lower socioeconomic status than earlier professional immigrants.[20] Korean Americans have slowly carved out a niche in the Hawai'i landscape.

Korean Americans in Hawai'i Today

According to U.S. Census data,[21] Koreans have consistently made up 2 percent of the total population in Hawai'i. According to the 1990 Census, there are 24,454 Koreans in Hawai'i. Literature on how Korean Americans are situated in Hawai'i is scarce, with few quantitative research contributions on the multi-ethnic community of Hawai'i.[22]

Haas offers the most recent and comprehensive book on multicultural Hawai'i, an anthology devoted to examining the sociocultural, economic, and political positions of the diverse ethnic populations in Hawai'i.[23] Haas states that Koreans in Hawai'i, along with Chinese and whites and Japanese, are considered privileged minority groups, but Koreans are second compared with the Chinese and whites, who are considered to be at the top of the ethnic hierarchy.[24] Koreans, Japanese, and African Americans are in the second tier, followed by Native Hawaiians, Filipinos, and Samoans at the bottom tier of the status hierarchy. Haas argues that the social position of Japanese, Chinese, and Koreans is largely due to the fact that these groups were the initial groups to immigrate and locate businesses in Hawai'i. Although the argument may account for Japanese and Chinese success, the number of Koreans who migrated during the plantation era was minimal, and as noted earlier, the majority of Koreans who immigrated after the 1965 Immigration Act were professionals. Thus, it is this that may account for the relative social success of Koreans in Hawai'i.

In his anthology, Okamura offers a rare glimpse of the social stratification and structural positions of the prominent ethnic groups in Hawai'i—in particular, African Americans, Chinese, Filipinos, Japanese, Native Hawaiians, Samoans, whites, and Koreans.[25] Although census analysis is not new to the field, Okamura's inclusion of Korean Americans and other minority groups[26] that have not been in the public discourse provides insight to the inter-ethnic relationships that exist in Hawai'i.

Occupational Positions of Korean Americans

In Hawai'i Korean Americans hold a variety of jobs, ranging from professional to blue-collar. However, the occupations differ for men and women. Korean males along with Chinese, Japanese, and whites are well represented in the executive/administrative and professional categories. Both Korean men and women are well represented in the technical, sales, and administrative support (TSAS) sector. According to the census, Korean men rate high in occupational ranking and success. Korean American men along with African American and Chinese are represented below the Hawai'i average in blue-collar work.[27]

Korean American women, however, are visible primarily in service work and are employed below parity as executives/administrators and professionals. Okamura states, "Korean women, who tend to be underrepresented in white collar work, are overly represented as service workers which also can be accounted for by the jobs held by immigrants, stereotypically as bar hostesses and restaurant workers."[28] Although there are a large number of Korean women in the hotel industry, working in housekeeping and janitorial services, the bar hostess image continues to be the predominant stereotype of Korean American women in Hawai'i. The occupational breakdown by gender and ethnicity in Hawai'i as of 1990 is presented in Table 1.

Income Level

As shown in Table 2, the Korean median family income is slightly below the state median family income. It is not surprising that the median Korean male income is above

TABLE 1

Occupational Distribution by Ethnic and Gender Group in Hawai'i, 1990

Total Male (277,735) Total Female (251,324)	Total (%)	Korean (%)	Black (%)	Caucasian (%)	Chinese (%)	Filipino (%)	Hawaiian (%)	Japanese (%)	Samoan (%)
	M F	M F	M F	M F	M F	M F	M F	M F	M F
Executive, administrative, and managerial (37,105, 30,802)	13.4 12.3	13.2 9.4	10.9 10.8	16.4 15.0	15.5 14.2	5.6 6.8	8.3 10.9	16.9 13.6	5.3 5.9
Professional specialty (32,821, 38,795)	11.8 15.4	10.4 8.2	9.5 12.9	16.8 21.5	14.6 15.3	3.3 6.2	6.3 10.9	17.6 10.4	7.4 8.3
Technical, sales, and administrative support (59,310, 113,244)	21.4 45.1	26.3 43.4	31.2 52.9	21.1 41.4	25.3 46.8	15.4 42.5	15.1 47.3	50.0 26.3	12.1 43.0
Precision production, craft, and repair (51,336, 4,182)	18.5 1.7	15.1 2.7	13.8 1.1	18.0 1.2	13.1 1.7	18.4 2.2	21.4 1.5	1.7 15.1	15.8 0.6
Operators, fabricators, and laborers (41,315, 11,839)	14.9 4.7	15.2 3.0	14.8 2.3	11.1 3.0	10.0 4.6	23.4 9.2	24.5 6.1	3.4 15.2	28.2 10.8
Service (44,047, 48,835)	15.9 19.4	17.2 32.1	19.0 19.1	12.8 16.7	19.6 16.7	25.3 29.7	19.3 22.4	12.7 17.2	28.0 29.9
Farming, forestry, and fishing (11,801, 3,527)	4.2 1.4	2.6 1.1	0.8 0.9	3.7 1.1	1.8 0.8	8.6 3.3	5.1 0.9	1.0 2.6	3.3 1.5

SOURCE: U.S. Census 1990

TABLE 2

Median Income by Ethnicity and Gender in Hawai'i

Ethnic Group	Family Income	Female Income	Male Income
Korean	$37,420	$17,023	$30,214
Black	$27,338	$14,478	$17,019
Caucasian	$41,878	$21,488	$26,881
Chinese	$48,518	$21,954	$31,889
Filipino	$41,955	$16,455	$21,871
Hawaiian	$37,960	$18,282	$26,029
Japanese	$52,982	$22,429	$33,501
Samoan	$23,914	$13,950	$19,901
Total	$43,176	$20,073	$27,147

SOURCE: U.S. Census 1990

the state median, considering that Korean males are well represented in professional and executive positions as well as in TSAS work. However, the median income of Korean American women falls below the state's median because Korean women are not well represented in professional and executive positions and are overly represented in the service sector. As a result of the low-income status of Korean women, the Korean median family income falls below the state's standard. Yet the census results do not take into account the entrepreneur families, who often have immediate family members working for low wages or no wages. Thus, this may also account for the low female and family income earnings in Hawai'i.

Education

According to the U.S. Census, the educational hierarchy is similar to the occupational and income scales. That is, whites and Chinese (25 years and older, male and female) are in the first tier, having the most bachelor's degrees;

Japanese, Koreans, and African Americans are in the second tier; and Filipino, Native Hawaiians, and Samoans are in the bottom tier in terms of attaining a college degree. The statistics are compiled in Table 3.

Among Korean Americans, a higher percentage of Korean males (25 years and older) have college degrees; in fact they are slightly above the Japanese. Korean females lag behind in their educational achievement, faring close to the Filipinas in Hawai'i.

Although recent researches and the U.S. Census provide a picture of how Koreans are situated in Hawai'i, it is difficult to determine exactly how many of the Korean Americans represented in the census are of the 1.5 generation. The lack of 1.5 generation representation in quantitative research is indicative of the "invisibility" of the 1.5ers in the Korean community itself. Much of how the island community views Korean Americans and how Korean 1.5ers view themselves is based on images of the

TABLE 3

Educational Attainment by Gender and Ethnic Group

Ethnic Group	Percentage 25 Years and Older with College Degrees	Percentage of Males 25–34 Years Old with College Degrees	Percentage of Females 25–34 Years Old with College Degrees
White	31.0	37.9	39.9
Chinese	30.0	33.3	39.8
Japanese	25.2	25.9	25.3
Korean	18.6	26.0	19.4
African American	15.2	10.1	17.3
Filipino	11.6	9.3	14.5
Native Hawaiian	9.1	9.5	8.9
Samoan	5.0	4.4	3.3

SOURCE: U.S. Census 1990

first generation-community. To date, there is limited academic research on the Korean community and none on 1.5ers in Hawai'i. The presentation of a Korean community is based on the visible businesses and organizations that exist on O'ahu, and the only official reference on the Korean American community is *The Korean Directory of Hawai'i*.

The Korean Directory of Hawai'i: Presentation of the Korean Community

The image and presentation of the Korean community is largely defined by the *Korean Directory of Hawai'i (Han in lok),* which attempts to show how the community is situated in Hawai'i. *Han in lok* is published annually by the United Korean Society (UKS) in Honolulu. This group, run by predominantly first-generation Koreans, maintains close ties to Korea and is looked to as the voice of the Korean American community. Thus, the UKS and the directory have so far constructed and presented what the Korean community is in Hawai'i.

According to *The Korean Directory of Hawai'i*, there are sixty-eight categories of Korean-owned/run businesses and 3,019 Korean American run businesses on O'ahu. From the various categories, ranging from upholstery work, to doctors, to taxi drivers, there are 445 businesses and organizations. Although the directory offers a vast listing of Korean American merchants and businesspeople, it is not comprehensive. Various restaurants, retail stores, and professional businesses are not included in the directory. In addition, only 14 of the 3,019 Korean Americans registered in the directory state that they are married to non-Koreans. Thus, a large number of Korean Americans married to non-Koreans are not included in the directory. Some of the reasons may be that businesses and organizations have closed and reopened under different names; some merchants did not want to be included in the directory for political or personal reasons, or did not want to pay for advertising; and the changing nature of the community makes it difficult to keep up with every new store, restaurant, or business that opens and closes. Still, the directory offers a general description of businesses and organizations in the Korean American community.

Due to large number of categories of business in the directory, I recoded the variables from sixty-eight categories to nine to reflect the types of businesses and services that are available in the community. According to the directory, 40 percent of the community businesses are restaurants, retail stores, food merchandisers (import/export), beauty salons, and health services (i.e., acupuncture and herbal medicine). Second is professional services (19.1 percent), which consists of doctors, clinics, dentists, optometrists, real estate agents, and insurance brokers. Third is the religious sector (15.1 percent), which consists of Methodist, Presbyterian, Catholic, and Buddhist churches and Protestant-oriented bookstores. The other businesses do not stand out as having a big impact on the community (see Table 4). It is not surprising that the island community often equates restaurants and churches with Korean Americans. Furthermore, as Okamura (1998b) points out, Korean American women in particular are often associated with hostess bars, which reinforces ethnic and gender stereotyping. Such images affect Korean American 1.5 ethnic identity as well as impressions of the Korean community itself. Discussion of the community's effect on the 1.5ers is covered in Chapter 6.

According to the directory, 86.3 percent of the businesses are located in Honolulu and 11.2 percent are in other areas of Oʻahu, with one on the Big Island. There were, however, eleven areas not listed in the directory, possibly the locations of privately owned businesses or consulting work (see Table 5).

When we look at the areas based on zip code, we see a similar picture of the Korean American community. Sixty-nine percent of the businesses are in what the GTE phone

TABLE 4

Frequency and Distribution of Korean American
Businesses in Hawai'i

Type of Business	Frequency	Percentage
Contract labor	50	11.2
Professional	85	19.1
Religious	67	15.1
Restaurant/retail	179	40.2
Media	5	1.1
Tourism	13	2.9
Education/school	15	3.4
Auto body shop	21	4.7
Other	10	2.2
Total	445	100

SOURCE: *The Korean Directory* 1998

TABLE 5

Locations of Korean American Businesses in Hawai'i

Area on O'ahu	Frequency	Percentage
Honolulu	384	86.3
Other	50	11.2
Total	434	97.5
Missing from total	11	2.5
Total	445	100

SOURCE: *The Korean Directory* 1998

book refers to as the "downtown" area of Makiki. It is
clear that a majority of the Korean businesses or what is
perceived as the Korean community is centered in
Honolulu, with few businesses and organizations in Aiea
and the Ewa area. Due to the heavy concentration of
Korean businesses and organizations in Honolulu, Korean
Americans work and live in Honolulu, and if they choose

to patronize Korean organizations or businesses, they must come to Honolulu.

There is, however, a growing Korean American population in Aiea and Salt Lake and in the new developments of Mililani and Kapolei, where housing costs are considered more reasonable. Makiki at one time was considered the Korean residential area; however, Koreans are scattered throughout the island. Though they work in Honolulu, they may live in the suburbs or in the outskirts of town. This is more consistent with national studies of Korean Americans, which state that although Korean Americans work in urban areas, they tend to live in the suburbs.[29] Although Korean Americans in Hawai'i are not geographically homogeneous, they currently live and work in "town" (Honolulu).

Businesses

As of 1997, restaurants and retail stores dominated the Korean American business community; professional businesses, such as attorneys, doctors, optometrists, insurance brokers, and real estate agents, fall close behind in numbers. Contracting has also been a growing area for the Korean American community. Manual labor jobs, such as contracting, painting, maintenance, and construction, are an area where Koreans have become a strong presence. However, this market is dominated by the first generation, with the professional field slowly being filled by the 1.5 and second generations. The trend seems to be that with each generation, the children are doing better and thus are opting to enter the professional market. Mr. Lee, a first-generation Korean American father and fisherman, explains:

> We come to America for a better life. I think we have done well. But when I talk to my friends about our [fishing] business, we know that after we are done, it's over. Our children are doing

their own thing, and they are not interested in continuing the family business. It's like the Japanese families. They used to run the fishing community here, and when the parents retired, they sold it to us and to the Vietnamese. Who knows who'll do it next; our children are moving on. I hope that our daughters will find good paying jobs.

Prior to the Koreans' penetration of the fishing industry, the Japanese dominated the scene; however, when the Sansei children came of working age, they opted for more professional occupations and chose not to continue their parents' fishing business. The Korean American fisherman states that similar things are occurring within the Korean fishing community. Although fathers would not mind their children taking over the family business, they urge their children to enter the professional market over taking blue-collar jobs. Hence, the community is seeing more young Korean American professionals than ever before.

Tourism

According to the *Korean Directory,* the tourist industry represents a small percentage of the business community. However, this is not an indication of the influence tourism has on the Korean American community. There were two main travel agencies in Honolulu that catered to Korean tourists and Korean Americans traveling to Korea. These two companies were flourishing with strong Korean currency and a growing interest among Korean Americans in conducting business in Korea. However, the day after the Korean economy crashed in early 1998, so did the travel agencies. Asiana, one of the main air carriers from Korea to Honolulu, announced that they would no longer be flying to Honolulu. In addition, the local Asiana travel agency closed its doors. The economic decline in Korea did not only affect the travel industry. In early 1998, retail stores in Sam Sung Plaza, which at one time marketed electronics strategically, changed their audience after larger electronic stores like Circuit City opened. Sam Sung renovated its stores into more Korean tourist–friendly department stores, with vans and buses full of eager Korean tourist buyers stopping at their doors. After putting such a large investment in products and renovation to its stores, Sam Sung Plaza, now named Euro Collection, is under the gun to rethink its marketing strategy to stay afloat.

Restaurants are also feeling the economic troubles of Korea. As with the retail stores, tourist vans and buses would cart large tourist groups after a difficult day of shopping into a familiar Korean restaurant. The restaurants now have to rethink their marketing strategy as they see fewer and fewer Korean tourists.

The most obviously affected are the hotels. In Honolulu, there is one hotel, the Waikiki Resort, owned by Korean Airlines, that caters to Korean tourists. Unlike other hotels, which market to the Japanese, Californians, and to some degree Europeans, the Waikiki Resort has focused most of its efforts on Korean tourists. The hotel staff are predominantly Korean-speaking Koreans. Sandy, a 1.5 generation front desk worker at the hotel, states that before Korea's economy crashed, the hotel consistently had an 80 percent occupancy rate, but lately they have been at 40 percent.

With the recent turn of events, it is difficult to predict the future of the Korean American business community. However, if Keʻeaumoku Street is any indicator of what is to come, we can expect to see more Korean-owned businesses popping up on Keʻeaumoku and its periphery.

Presently, the image of the Korean American community is based on the businesses of the first generation, which deters the 1.5 generation from investing and participating in the Korean American community as it is currently presented. An emerging problem of the Korean American community in Hawaiʻi is the lack of central leadership. Like Korean American communities in the continental United States, there is no one to integrate, coordinate, and direct various community activities and to address the concerns and needs of all Korean American generations; thus, when problems occur, the parties are unable to handle them internally and end up taking disputes to court.[30] Today, with more Korean Americans achieving higher education, the children of immigrants are more likely to work outside the family-owned business and to pursue their own career goals. Roger, a 35-year-old lawyer, states, "I feel that I can go real far in life, and in Hawai'i I won't be able to do that. I can see myself in DC, or even in Korea." The Korean American 1.5 generation, unlike their parents, are able to use their professional degrees without the language barrier problem. By pursuing their own careers, they may leave their parents for locations where employment is available. With jobs located across the United States, Korean American extended families may quickly turn into conjugal families. In addition, 1.5ers are more likely to have their own residence than to live with their parents in their adult years. They are also less likely to spend time with their grandparents, let alone live with them under one roof. The type of work sought, therefore, will contribute to the changing face of Korean American families in future generations.

The face of the Korean American community shifted greatly after the late 1980s economic success of Korea. As more Korean Americans strengthened ties to Korea, an increased number of Korean-owned businesses, investments, and import/export operations emerged. The transpacific ties have helped maintain a sense of diasporic identity for many Korean Americans, who keep constant ties to issues and people in Korea. Members of the community acknowledge that currently, the image of the Korean American community is based on first-generation leadership, and that image needs to change if Koreans in Hawai'i wish to branch out to the local community. However, to establish ties with non-Koreans, they must first deconstruct the Korean American community to address the ethnic and generational boundaries that the community has established. Race relations in Hawai'i are unique and affect interpersonal relationships, family dynamics, and the overall sense of ethnic identity. One must examine the culture of Hawai'i and its people to truly understand the situation in which Koreans negotiate their ethnic identity in everyday situations.[31]

Hawai'i's Culture and What It Means to Be Local

The experience of Korean child immigrants growing up in Hawai'i is significantly different from that of 1.5ers growing up anywhere in the continental United States. Clearly, the geographic location where one is raised will set in that community's own qualities of culture. However, what Korean Americans growing up in different parts of the continental United States have in common is that race relations are based on the legacy of white supremacy. Immigrants and even second- and third-generation Asian Americans are seen as foreigners, regardless of their occupational status, language abilities, and education. If you are not white, you're a foreigner.[32]

Craig, a 29-year-old banker, states, "Being white means that you assume everyone is like you. Your impression is everyone's impression. Even when there are five blacks there, you assume your perception of the world is shared by all." Yen Le Espiritu's book *Asian American Panethnicity* explores the construction of large-scale affiliations in which diverse ethnic groups of Asian descent submerge their differences and assume a common pan-Asian identity.

Jon Okamura, on the other hand, argues that there are no Asian Americans in Hawai'i. In "Why There Are No Asian Americans in Hawai'i," Okamura discusses the fusion of local identity due to a series of economic, political, and social struggles that took place with respect to Hawaiʻi-Japanese investment, the increasing population of tourists, and the Native Hawaiian sovereignty movement.[33] "These and other factors reveal a sense of local identity that is not solely premised on a common ethnic or racial background, but on the tensions between insiders and outsiders."[34] Wayne Wooden's books *What Price Paradise* and *Return to Paradise* examine the notion of in-group/out-group status as a mean of achieving local status.[35] It is important to look at the history of Hawaiʻi as to how the term *local* made its way into mainstream discussions.

Hawaiʻi inherited a new oligarchy system as a result of colonization; however, the influence of the indigenous people of Hawaiʻi on colonized Hawaiʻi remained. Although white Americans took the land away from the indigenous people, the racial composition of the islands prevented the ruling group from dominating the ethnic workers in number. In fact, some argue that Hawaiʻi is the one state where no ethnic group dominates.

During the plantation era, plantation owners recruited Japanese, Chinese, Korean, and Filipinos to keep up with the demand for sugar from Hawaiʻi.[36] These groups constructed a pidgin language so that they could communicate and in the process created a new community. The plantation life became symbolic of the heart and sweat that many immigrants put into creating a life in Hawaiʻi. Some argue that one must have ties to the plantation period to be considered local. The term *local,* however, was not used in popular Hawaiʻi culture until the infamous Massie trial. John Rosa writes of how the term *local* was used in the press to distinguish between the Massies, a white military couple, and the alleged perpetrators of an attack on Mrs. Massie, a group of Japanese and Hawaiian boys. Subsequently, *local* was used to refer to any nonwhite resident born and raised in Hawaiʻi, and since most of the nonwhite residents of Hawaiʻi were plantation workers and their children, its class implications were obvious.[37] The concept of local is very similar to the concept of American in the continental United States. Indigeneous groups would argue that the true Americans are Native Americans, and some argue that the true Locals are Native Hawaiians. As one listserv member writes,

> *I think that for those who are Hawaiian, they are*   **45**
> *local but more importantly, they are native. To*
> *me, local refers to "local-ity." I feel that those*
> *who live here and accept the mixtures of cultures*
> *and traditions, they could be considered local.*
> *The funny thing is that sometimes I'll be watching*
> *TV and see an Asian character with fairly dark*
> *skin and wonder if that person is local. I believe*
> *that a local identity has evolved into one with*
> *more Asian physical characteristics. Of course,*
> *this is just my perspective but it seems that*
> *Caucasians would have more difficulty associat-*
> *ing themselves (and being accepted) as a "local."*

Although people may refer to Koreans who have lived in the United States for a prolonged period of time as Americans, people in Hawai'i refer to Koreans who were raised there and can pass as Hawai'i born as local. Yumiko Oliver Richardson began writing about Sansei women in Hawai'i; however, she quickly recognized that being local overshadowed being third generation. She states, "For Sansei women, the prominent aspect of life on the islands, was their uniqueness and distinctiveness in relation to local culture."[38] For those living on the islands, the idea of "local" has distinguished them from outside groups impinging on their society and has also created a sense of cohesion among the ethnic groups living on the islands.

Another person on the listserv writes,

> *To me local is a culture, it is the ability to under-*
> *stand that my culture is unique and that everyone*
> *including my people (Filipinos) have attributed*
> *to. I take my slippers off when I enter someone's*

house, most of my neighbors or people who are much older than me I call "antie" or "uncle," I played Hawaiian-style football when I was young, and I love my Kamaboko slippers. Although many of us may have not experienced a struggle of sovereignty, I still find myself proud of where I'm from.[39]

Local culture offers an ethnic option for Asian immigrants that is not readily available to them in the continental United States. For 1.5 generation Korean Americans in particular, it is possible to switch among Korean, Korean American, and local identities depending on the situation. Being local provides them with an opportunity to fit in and at times blend in with a group that has a social and political history on the islands. The unique sociopolitical structure of the islands helps create a different kind of race relations. However, the racial stratification in Hawai'i is not that different from the situation in the continental United States. The location merely offers Korean Americans a choice in their ethnic identity.

3

SOCIAL CONSTRUCTION
OF ETHNIC IDENTITY

There has been an emergence of theories to address ethnic identity formation. One distinction in particular has shaped the way we look at how ethnic minorities adapt or acculturate in the United States: the notion of a fixed versus a fluid identity. Assimilation theorists argue that minority immigrant groups will shed their culture and replace it with the mainstream society's culture. Thus, all groups will eventually become one group with one culture, and physical differences will be difficult to identify due to mass "melting" among the people.[1] The notion of a fixed identity was widely accepted largely because of the invisibility of people of color in the dominant race discourse. As far as the early theorists were concerned, since early European/Anglo immigrants had assimilated and become "white," the same fate was inevitable for all "Americans." Some ethnic minority groups have bought into the idea of a fixed and assimilated identity. Hurh argues that the young generations of Korean Americans are considered 100% American, for many speak English fluently, are bilingual, and some do not even speak Korean.[2] Such a notion of being "American" suggests equal status or equal opportunities. However, this is far from the truth. Ethnic minorities have constructed a new set of ethnic options that helps them navigate the tenuous racial terrains in the United States.

Waters' study of ethnic and racial identities adopted by second-generation adolescents of West Indian and Haitian origin in New York City discerned a form of adaptation, but in this case breaking out of the immigrant circle meant embracing an African American identity, which was perceived by their parents as downward assimilation. Parents' social class and background, social networks, family structure, and the type of school the child attended were influential in determining the manner in which the youths tried to shed their immigrant status.[3]

Much like the case with Korean Americans in Hawaiʻi, the choice of passing as local is seen as undesirable to some families of middle- to upper-class status. However, it is not necessarily viewed in this light by working-class families or families who have an appreciation for local culture. The idea of identifying with African Americans as "downward assimilation" has much to do with internalized racism toward black Americans. Those who have respect and appreciation for the struggles of African American people would most likely hold a different perception of identifying as African American. What is important about Waters' study is that it illustrates how ethnic minority youth look for a group where they can belong, and since their racial features demarcate them from the dominant white society, they seek other groups that closely resemble them.

Mary Waters' optional situation theory addresses the social inequities that exist for ethnic minorities, which not only make it difficult for them to be accepted by mainstream society, but also make them disadvantaged in their own communities. She points out that ethnic options are more available to whites than to ethnic minorities. Ethnic minorities are visibly branded as a particular racial group and are seen by others as an ethnic minority before anything else. Waters' assertions validate the analysis of Asian Americans being perceived as foreigners or outsiders regardless of how many generations of their families have been in the United States. However, Korean Americans and other people of Asian descent in Hawaiʻi have options similar to those of the whites that Waters speaks of. Due to the locality of Hawaiʻi and the dynamics of race relations, some Korean Americans who have been in Hawaiʻi for a long time and who have adapted to the ways of the islands can often pass as local. Consequently, some Korean Americans of the 1.5 and second generations have the option of choosing their Korean, local, Asian American, or 1.5 ethnic identity.

If we are to dispute the notions of melting pot, assimilation, and acculturation, which are used interchangeably, we must also challenge the idea that being local means only one thing. The historical, cultural, and generational influence of Korean Americans in the dominant local culture has created more choices for Korean Americans. In the continental United States, Korean Americans may pass as members of another Asian ethnic group, but they are still seen as the minority. When Korean Americans appear more "Americanized," they are seen as being "whitewashed." Pressure from peers and parents can tighten the tug-of-war of ethnic and national loyalties that contributes to a sense of marginality. Thus, a young Korean woman feels the sting of being called a "Twinkie" by co-ethnics during her freshmen year in college "just because I grew up in a white suburb and was a cheerleader," while her mother will not let her forget that she has to marry a Korean. However, in Hawaiʻi, when Korean Americans are perceived as local, they are seen as part of the dominant group.

Minority groups have praised the concept of looking beyond a person's skin color and "biological genes," and have embraced the notion of cultural heritage as a distinction between minorities. However, the concept of ethnicity has itself become a heated debate. What exactly is "cultural heritage," and what does that have to do with minority identification? How about those who are "mixed"?

What about second-, third-, and fourth-generation minorities? The very idea of cultural heritage, once embraced by many, has faced critical attacks on the very nature of what it is to be ethnic. J. C. Mitchell early on attempted to discuss perceptions of ethnicity and ethnic behavior.[4] Although ethnicity is a state of mind, there is a distinction between commonsense and analytical/intellectual understandings of ethnicity. The idea of "ethnic group" soon became manifested as what many call "ethnic identity" today.

50

Increasingly, ethnic identity is recognized as being fluid and contextual. More and more theorists agree that, particularly among minority groups, the notion of ethnic identity is constructed and reconstructed depending on the situation.[5] Individuals' and groups' attempts to address ethnic boundaries and meanings of ethnicity are best understood as a constant exchange between individual identity and group organization.[6] The way we construct our ethnic identity is the result of structure and agency, the interchange between ethnic groups and the larger society. Behaviors and actions of ethnic groups are a product of the social and political environment.[7] The idea of ethnicity as a fluid process can be used to examine the resocialization experiences of Korean American 1.5ers.

Social construction theory states that members of a group have their own position on how they should act in a given situation, and then later shift to collective action. For example, the experiences of Korean American 1.5ers help shape a collective 1.5 consciousness. Social construction theory is exceptionally useful to undertaking research on Korean American 1.5 ethnic identity because it assumes that ethnic group identities are negotiated, created, and questioned.[8] The constructionist perspective contrasts with that of assimilationists, who view identity as fixed and uncompromising. When immigrant groups become American, assimilationists argue that the groups have conformed to the dominant group. Hence, such views portray the immigrant experience of becoming American as the final stage. Social construction, however, concerns itself with the individual's point of view as well as the nature of the situation in which collective action is constructed.[9] I have selected certain aspects of the theory—social process and identity options—to analyze the processes by which 1.5 generation Korean Americans in Hawai'i negotiate between being Korean and being "Korean American"/"local."

It is not the case that Korean 1.5ers are in one instance immigrants and with time become more "Americanized/local." Based on their experiences, meanings are considered through a process of interpretation during which they take into account the relevant objects in the situation they confront, including the activities of others, the anticipated activities of others, conventional definitions of the situation, past experience, goals, interests, values, and so on.

The key idea is that Korean 1.5ers themselves create their identity based on the way they have been treated by other Koreans and non-Koreans, such as parents, peers, and teachers. Self-identification is also affected by the evaluations of others at the micro and macro levels, as well as by the opportunities and constraints regarding self-definition imposed by them. Furthermore, child immigrants are affected not only by the interactions but also by the meanings he or she attaches to the interactions.

The investigation of race and ethnicity in cities is used to address questions about choices and preferences, social distances, and the related phenomena of inclusion, exclusion, and maintenance of boundaries that demarcate "us and them."[10] Thus, it is important to look at 1.5 ethnic groups in terms of how they negotiate generational and ethnic boundaries among themselves, "Americans," "Locals," and their first-generation parents.

The experiences of young Korean immigrants are significantly different from those of their parents, and through the process of deculturation from Korean tradition, they can assert a "separate" group identity, different from those of the first and second generations. This assertion of a separate group identity may be valued in and of itself as well as as a strategy to improve the self-esteem of members and enhance their competitiveness with regard to the universal values sought by all or most members of the society at large.[11] Despite such a possible resolution, this issue is still under ongoing debate because it raises questions having to do with the extent to which societies require sources of consensus and solidarity that transcend ethnic and other.[12] "In respect to ethnicity optionalists contend that the ethnic group only exists when members are conscious of belonging to a group."[13]

The optional-situational concept of ethnic identity does not ignore the fact that ethnicity is created not only by the self, but by others as well. It is also important to note that powerful groups may try and may succeed in creating identities for a group not felt by its members, as was the case for those assimilated Jews who saw themselves as Germans and not as Jews during the Nazi era. The concept of identity options makes clear the necessity of investigating why and how identities do or do not get constructed in situations of varying degrees of constraint.[14] What is too often forgotten, however, is that no matter what their focus—be it descent, physical appearance, nationality, gender, disability, occupation, age, class, or whatever—our human capacity to resist these forces is not only immense but tends to increase as conditions become ever more severe.

To summarize, the optional-situational approach conceives of ethnic identity as an ongoing process in which individuals or groups see themselves, and define themselves with respect to others, in many different ways. Among the factors that influence how groups construct their identities at any time is the situation that they confront, including their goals, the constraints inherent in the activities and collective definitions of others, and the positive and negative value they assume a particular identity will confer. Ethnic identity, although subject to constraints, is changeable and self-interested. For example, Korean American 1.5ers internalize immigrant Korean stereotypes of the larger society and therefore feel ashamed of being Korean. However, these negative views change when they meet other 1.5ers who give them reason to be proud of their ethnicity.

Second, the optional-situational perspective treats the emergence of new identities, such as the Korean American 1.5ers, as normal features of multi-ethnic societies. Third, because it is based on the process of collective definition, the optional-situational approach to ethnic identity is able to anticipate and deal with changes in self-definition and redefinition of others as an instance of emergent meaning and as a usual feature of collective life. Finally, the framework allows groups to switch and choose their identities at a given time. It is likely that Korean American 1.5ers will under certain conditions wish to leave their Korean immigrant identity behind and appear to be more American or local.

Theories and Models of Ethnic Identity Development

There has been a variety of literature on ethnic identity—from the perspective of minority groups to how the ecology affects ethnic identity. In this section, I will discuss theories and models of ethnic identity development—models that demonstrate how minority groups develop a sense of identity and theories on why they may do so. In addition, I will review literature on how family and community ethnically socialize minority groups. Ethnic identity development models combined with social construction theory provide a framework to examine the experiences of 1.5ers in constructing a Korean American 1.5 ethnic identity.

Phinney (1990) argues for more comprehensive studies measuring a range of components of ethnic identity. One important aspect concerns the way one defines oneself. This aspect is important because it locates the individual within a particular social and cultural framework and because it may differ from one's ethnic group membership. Subjects do not have to define themselves in terms of their ethnic origin. For instance, people may feel that a single ethnic label, whether chosen or imposed, is inaccurate inasmuch as they feel part of two or more groups. Verkuyten and Kwa (1994) distinguish four types of self-definition based on identification with one's own minority group and the majority group: dissociative, assimilative, acculturative, and marginal. All four were found to be present among minority youth in the Netherlands, showing that self-identification among minority youth is a two-dimensional process. In addition, the different types of self-identification showed a clear pattern of differences for self-esteem, self-concept stability, and life satisfaction. Minority youths who identified predominantly with the majority group (assimilative) or neither with their own minority group nor with the majority group (marginal) scored lower on these aspects of psychological well-being than subjects who identified predominantly with their own group (dissociative) or with both the minority and majority group (acculturative or bicultural). Though the authors' four types of self-identification are used to describe individuals, such patterns of differences can be attributed to ethnic groups such as the Korean American 1.5ers. Through the socialization process 1.5ers can identify with all four types; however, the types are not mutually exclusive. The 1.5ers can identify with the four types during the process of constructing an ethnic identity and may alter their identification with varying situations.

Verkuyten and Kwa's theory predicts that in a situation where group boundaries are seen as impermeable and relatively stable, minority groups will stress their ethnic identity in order to counteract a negative social identity.

However, an additional explanation is put forward by Hutnik (1991), who argues that attention should not be paid only to the minority aspect of identity but also to the ethnic aspect. What should not be underestimated are the powerful forces at work in ethnic groups themselves. These groups are endowed with a culture, tradition, and structure of their own, providing people with a sense of ethnic dignity. Ethnic group members do not have to look elsewhere for the construction of a positive ethnic identity since they have their own rich culture and tradition. In addition, for many minority groups around the world, and especially for children of immigrants, there is the question of how to deal with conflicting cultural norms, values, and demands of the majority and minority cultures. Although 1.5 generation Korean Americans may feel marginalized and ashamed of their ethnicity, they also express positive characteristics and views of Koreans. The 1.5ers may internalize negative stereotypes, but they simultaneously assert positive group image as well.

IDENTITY DEVELOPMENT

The early work on minority identity development was primarily done by African American intellectuals.[15] Hall, Freedle, and Cross (1972) described their identity development model as the "Negro-to-black conversion experience," consisting of four stages. The first stage is the pre-encounter stage, where blacks are "programmed to view and think of the world as being non-black, anti-black, or the opposite of Black." In the second, the encounter stage, the black person acknowledges being black and becomes aware of what being black means in mainstream society. In the third, the immersion stage, the black person rejects all that is not black and becomes immersed in the black culture. In the fourth, the internalization stage, the black person finds inner security and begins to focus on larger issues rather than being self-absorbed.

This model demonstrates how African Americans initially attempt to assimilate to the dominant white culture; then, after being rejected by whites, they acknowledge the physical difference of being black, become angered and reject the dominant culture, and attempt to educate others and better their own cultural heritage. However, the model is too simplistic and unilinear. It does not account for the complexity of time and place or the varying experiences of African Americans, nor does it account for those African Americans who are now part of mainstream society and how they deal with being surrounded by those people they reject. Minorities take on much more sophisticated methods of identifying themselves, and not all involve the total rejection of another group in order to feel better about one's own group. Such analysis patronizes the African American experience and their ability to identify themselves racially. Moreover, this type of model perpetuates the dominant stereotypical view of race relations as a black-and-white issue. It does not account for the varying interethnic conflicts that occur in many inner cities, the social and political factors that may contribute to such self-labeling, or identity development in other minority groups, such as immigrants.

Atkinson, Morten, and Sue (1993) attempt to extend the identification model to represent all minorities rather than just African Americans. Their "minority identity development model" includes five stages. In the first stage, conformity, minorities devalue their own ethnicity and ethnic group as well as other minority groups while admiring and appreciating the dominant white group. In the second stage, dissonance, minority groups face inner conflict between the appreciation and depreciation of themselves and their group. Furthermore, they begin to feel a sense of shared experience and history with other minority groups and question the dominant views of minority hierarchy. In the third stage, resistance and immersion, minorities begin to appreciate themselves and the group, yet they face conflicting feelings of empathy for other minority experiences and feelings of culture-centrism. At this stage, they begin to depreciate the dominant group. In the fourth stage, introspection, individuals begin to question the basis of self- and group appreciation and become concerned with their ethnocentric basis for judging other minorities and their depreciating views toward the dominant group. In the final stage, synergetic articulation and awareness, individuals appreciate themselves, their group, and other minority groups, and selectively appreciate the dominant group.

The ethnic identity model of Atkinson and colleagues does not differ much from that of Hall and colleagues; it has merely added the last stage of appreciation and selective appreciation for the dominant group. Both models, however, fail to clearly demonstrate the psychological, social, and political processes of identity development. First, the models assume that minorities will go through the five stages, when in fact, many may never encounter any of the stages. Second, the models insinuate a psychological transformation without taking into account political policies that may affect behaviors and attitudes. Finally, the models, although addressing the issue of assimilation, do not take into account the notion of biculturality, the ability to adapt to both cultures. The authors discuss the process of development without taking into consideration the role of agency, such as the role of parents in ethnically socializing Korean youths. Again, such theories negate the presence of immigrant children in the process of learning a new culture as they concurrently construct a new identity to adapt to the host society as well as their traditional culture.

One of the central issues for adolescents is to settle on some picture of who and what they are. Uncertainty about self-concept seems to be at its peak during adolescence, when all that was taken for granted about the self in childhood becomes questioned. Doubt and uncertainties are introduced, not only because of dramatic physical and physiological changes but also because of altered social experiences and changing demands from society. The result can be a relatively unstable, shifting self-concept that is a major aspect of what Erikson (1950) calls "identity confusion."

While Korean American 1.5ers go through many of these stages, they also gain a sense of 1.5 ethnic identity consciousness. Although the stages are applicable to 1.5ers, it is external influences, such as school, non-Korean peers, and media, during the process of ethnic identity formation that help construct a collective 1.5 ethnic identity.

FAMILY AND ETHNIC SOCIALIZATION

Social scientists state that the family is the strongest agent of socialization; consequently, there have been a vast number of studies conducted on the relationship between parents and children. Parents are expected to teach their children the norms, values, beliefs, traditions, and everything else that is a part of their society. Minority parents have the double burden of socializing their children to the mainstream culture and at the same time socializing them about their cultural heritage.

Socializing children is a difficult task, but what does it mean to ethnically socialize a child? Focusing on one's ethnicity has been a development primarily triggered by the civil rights movement; Caucasian movements to ethnically socialize their children to be Italian, French, or Irish, for example, are rare. The sensitization to ethnicity is a direct result of the failure of assimilation theory. Minority parents are aware that in the United States, people are not all treated equally, and that once one passes the United States citizenship test, one is not seen like other Americans. For minority immigrants, the label of minority remains, and with it comes harsh social and political realities.

For many immigrant families, the words typically used to describe the impact of immigration are "breakdown," "increased conflict," and "increased enmeshment," which affect the immigrant family as a whole.[16] For some parents, there is a reordering of roles; parents may depend on their school-age children for translation help, children may be asked to be the primary caregivers for their infant siblings while their parents are working, and parents may practice close monitoring and overprotection of their children.[17] Thus, in the United States, immigrant Korean parents teach their children Korean culture and what it means to be Korean while simultaneously creating a sense of what it means to be Korean American. Needless to say, the stress of migration, changes in parenting styles, and a new place affect children to some degree, but what is it that minority children have the most difficult time with? Aside from issues of autonomy, identity crisis, and peer influence, these children have the burden of coping with conflicting cultural values and parents who may disapprove of their means of acculturation.[18] So what are minority parents to do? Do they stress the importance of belonging to the mainstream culture, as many assimilation theorists would suggest, or do they ignore the dominant culture and take pride in their own ethnic culture, as some minority models may argue? The choices are not black and white for immigrant parents in general and for Korean American parents in particular, who teach their children about both Korean and American values, thus creating a sense of Korean American culture.

In studying the effects of ethnic identity on youth, Phinney, Chavira, and Williamson (1992) found that among high school and college students, integration, that is, the idea that ethnic minority groups should maintain their own cultural traditions but also learn to get along in mainstream American society, was highly endorsed as having a positive effect on youths' self-esteem and academic achievements. I would add that it is the acceptance of both cultures by the minority children that will have positive effects. If 1.5ers have pride in being only Korean or "American," but not both, the outcome of how they feel about themselves will be different. Thus, ethnic identity has a strong influence on the development of children.

Parents who socialize their children for living in a diverse culture have children with a stronger sense of ethnic identity.[19] In fact, children who are aware of social diversity and challenges tend to do better in school than those who are not socialized to diversity.[20] It is clear that parents need to understand the social problems that children encounter and the effects these experiences have on their lives. Educating minority children about the dominant culture also means educating them about discrimination, prejudice, racism, and inequality.[21] Unfortunately, not all parents have the time to educate their children on social inequalities. Asian Americans learn about such injustices firsthand.

Acculturating a child to the vast differences in a new culture is a psychosocial process.[22] The parent and child must both learn a new language and norms of social interaction, wrestle with new values and beliefs, and relate to family members who may have chosen a different mode of acculturation. Chiu and colleagues (1992) suggest that immigrant children are more distressed than nonimmigrant children, experiencing lower self-esteem, poor concentration, and nervousness. Yet this is not uniformly agreed upon. Some researchers suggest that the length of residence in the host country influences the symptoms.[23] It is unclear at this point how Korean American 1.5ers are affected by stress. Possibly as a result of the language barrier, Korean Americans who migrate at an older age may not be able to hide their Korean accent, whereas younger immigrants may be able to present themselves as more "Korean American"/"local." In the process of becoming Korean American, 1.5ers are influenced by family, the larger society, and other 1.5ers on what it means to be Korean, Korean American/local and Korean American 1.5 generation.

It is evident that we cannot generalize the effects of migration, and that each minority group has to be considered individually. We have to consider how parents and family are socializing the children and examine the child's role in the family. A Korean American 1.5er who is responsible for translating for the family and taking care of the younger kids obviously is more likely to experience external stress more than an "average" 12-year-old child. Thus, the experiences of immigrants should not be typified.

For other immigrant families, the passing down of their culture becomes key to their own livelihood. Nazli Kibria (2002) writes of how 1.5 and second-generation Korean Americans and Chinese Americans share their parents' wish to maintain a part of their heritage. "There are some things about being Korean or Chinese that they would like to pass down to their children, most notably the values, emphasis of family, work, and education. . . . Distilled ethnicity, then, suggests a passed-down ethnicity that meshes easily with established notions of a mainstream middle-class American lifestyle and sensibility" (p. 162).

Kibria shows how Asian Americans identify with the idea of being ethnic Americans. They see themselves as part of the long-standing experiences of immigration and ethnicity. But at the same time, as racial minorities they are often frustrated in this identification, a situation that drives them to recognize the gap between their own situation and that of white Americans. Kibria suggests that further developments may resolve this situation—especially the emergence of a new kind of pan–Asian American identity that would complement the Chinese or Korean American identity rather than replace it. Some may argue that distinguishing ethnic differences in children perpetuates the ethnic segregation of people in the United States. As Lisa Kim, a 1.5er who works in the travel industry, asks, "Why can't we all be American instead of separating ourselves as *blank* American?" Lisa believes, like many others, that this separation of ethnic groups only flames the fires of discrimination, inequality, and racism. What is interesting is that many of us in "mainstream" society forget the social and political history of the minority struggle to be "accepted, to "fit in," and to "belong." Being alienated by the dominant culture is an experience shared by almost all minority groups. But the notion of "America" as a host to multicultural differences is ideological and unreal. In the Constitution, "we the people" referred not to the people of the United States but to the white men of the United States. Women and people of color were not included in the equation.

It is understandable with this kind of history why parents would want to socialize their children about their ethnic identity and what it means to be a minority in the United States. Without a clear understanding of what one's ethnic identity means, it is difficult to interact in a society that has historically been bitten by the "racist" bug. It is in the best interest of the child to understand the challenges in the mainstream society in order to prepare for what may lie ahead. Is this not the responsibility of all parents, to ensure that their children are well equipped to weather what may be in store for them? The shared history of minorities is one of the reasons for ethnic self-identification, to end the alienation of being different, to be proud of one's culture, and to contribute to society as a minority owning one's ethnicity.

The closest attempt to study the influence of family, peers, education, and work on Korean American identity was conducted by Kim, Kim, and Hurh (1991). Kim and Hurh (1993) state that Korean immigrants have syncretically adapted by combining the traditional Korean family system, which they refer to as the extended conjugal family, with the industrial way of life in the United States. The authors suggest that by restructuring their belief system, families develop a maturational perspective firmly rooted in the changing reality of Korean immigrants in the United States. Kim, Kim, and Hurh (1991) suggest that a revived expectation of filial piety retains the cultural norms, but a modification of it allows intergenerational relationships in Korean immigrant families to adapt to current life conditions. The change in the family structure may prove to be confusing for particularly young American-raised (1.5 generation) and American-born (second generation) children. They may initially feel marginalized between the two cultures as a result of trying to reconstruct their identity to fit both American and Korean ethnicities. Although first- and second-generation Korean Americans may experience an extended conjugal family system, it is unclear what type of family will emerge for third, fourth, and future Korean American generations. As more Korean American women intermarry, our understanding of the Korean American family is apt to change.[24] Moreover, the intercultural influence of a biracial couple is also likely to affect the child's identity and the dynamics in the family.

63

The merging of Western and Korean influences has created a Korean American family. Yet the effects on children cause the youth to become marginalized. Although marginalization is part of socialization in the American culture, the 1.5ers gain a sense of collective 1.5 ethnic identity and embrace the uniqueness of being 1.5 Korean American. As they meet other 1.5ers, they gain a sense of pride in being Korean American and they consciously use their bilingual and bicultural abilities to their advantage rather than being confused by them.

COMMUNITY AND ETHNIC SOCIALIZATION

Although the family is often seen as the primary source of ethnic identity socialization, there are other agents of socialization that are just as influential. Bronfenbrenner's (1979, 1986) theory of the ecological model posits a direct impact of the environment on the functioning of individuals, families, and communities. He utilizes the ecological model to explain the concept of "person in environment." Much like social construction theory, the ecological model examines the multilayered sociocultural influences on an individual. Bronfenbrenner defines the ecology of human development as the "scientific study of the progressive, mutual accommodation between an active growing human being and the changing properties of the immediate settings in which the developing person lives, as the process is affected by relations between these settings, and by the larger context in which the settings are embedded."[25] This definition points to three central ideas: (1) The individual is not only affected by the environment but is constantly negotiating and transforming the setting in which he or she participates. (2) Sinwce the individual also affects the environment, the interaction between person and environment is viewed as bidirectional, that is, categorized by reciprocity. (3) There is no single immediate setting that influences an individual's development process; rather, the interconnections between settings as well as external influences are included. Thus, the ecological model is conceived topologically as a nested arrangement of concentric structures, each inside the next, "like a set of Russian dolls."[26] Bronfenbrenner refers to these structures as the microsystem, mesosystem, exosystem, and macrosystem.

The microsystem is the pattern of activities, roles, and interpersonal relationships experienced by the developing individual in a given setting where people engage in face-to-face or one-on-one interaction. A central core of development for an individual is the family, yet one can also look at the microsystem of a social organization. In an organization, there are roles and expectations for each member. For example, in the Korean Jaycees, a voluntary organization, there are the officers, board members, and general members. Although the Jaycee members' roles are explicit in the social organization, there are various relationships that can be observed at this level, such as president–officers, board members–general members, and general members–general members. As Bronfenbrenner points out, the micro level is phenomenological in that settings are perceived by the people who participate in the process and experience the situation.

The mesosystem is the interrelation among two or more settings in which the developing individual actively participates. The mesosystem can also be considered a system of microsystems. It is formed whenever a person makes an ecological transition (moves into a new setting). For example, when one goes to work, he or she makes the transition from family to work. The experiences at home can affect one's behavior at work, and the experience at work can affect one's behavior at home. The mesosystem influences operate in both directions between the principal settings in which development occurs.

Some settings can affect an individual's development even if the individual is not directly participating in the settings. The exosystem refers to one or more settings that do not involve the individual directly but affect the individual's development. For Korean American 1.5ers, their sense of ethnic pride occurs not only within themselves but also in the community. The ethnic stereotypes of Koreans in Hawai'i as "bar hostess," "materialistic," "rude," and "hot-tempered" may have a lateral effect on the psychological development of 1.5ers and their sense of ethnic identity.[27] In other words, the exosystem refers to the environment external to the developing person. There are three exosystems that are likely to affect the development of the child, primarily through their influence in the family process: parent's work, parent's network of friends, and community influence. The non-Korean community's influence, although significant, has not been addressed in reference to its influence on ethnic identity formation.

The macrosystem "refers to consistencies, in the form and content of lower order systems (micro, meso, exo) that exist, or could exist at the level of subculture or the culture as a whole along with belief systems or ideology underlying such consistencies."[28] In other words, a macrosystem refers to the structural elements in a society that serve as a "blueprint" for an individual's behavior. For example, the larger society influences Korean American 1.5ers' impressions of what it means to be Korean American/local. Perceptions of immigrant stereotypes affect how 1.5ers view and interact with other Korean Americans. In addition, notions of what a Korean American family should be, based on the larger society's impressions, affect how 1.5ers interact with their parents and siblings in their homes.

In 1986, Bronfenbrenner added the chronosystem as a designated research model that examines the environment's influence on a person's development over time. The simplest form of chronosystem centers on the individual's life transition. He states that there are two life transitions that individuals go through: normative (e.g., school entry, puberty, work, marriage, retirement) and nonnormative (e.g., death, divorce, moving, winning the lottery). Bronfenbrenner states that such changes occurring over time serve as the impetus for developmental change.

The ecological model thus views the "person in environment," where people interact with many systems at a time and the individual is viewed in relationship with the various systems. Moreover, it takes into account changes over time not only within the person but also within the environment that permit analysis of the dynamic relation between these two processes. Although Bronfenbrenner's model is used to examine the "person in environment," the model can also be used to examine the influences on groups. The ecological levels influence group identity, including ethnic identity. However, what is lacking in this model is the process of development. By incorporating this process and the external influences in examining ethnic identity formation, we can begin to examine the process by which 1.5 Korean Americans construct their ethnic identity.

Germain examines the role of community support systems in influencing individuals. He differentiates between informal and formal communities. He conceptualizes informal communities as systems that develop spontaneously, that is, "networks of face-to face personal relationships of an intimate and affiliate nature based on sentiment."[29] Informal communities interact at the level of who they are and not what they do. "Families typify informal systems, which also comprise adult friendship groups, children's play groups, and informal support networks."[30] Formal communities are characterized by hierarchical levels of authority—for example, job specializations; replaceable organizational roles; relationships based on what people do; and rules, policies, and procedures of work operations. Formal communities are thus characterized as complex bureaucratic organizations ranging from being centralized and hierarchical to those that are less formal. Often, the formal organization does not address the interpersonal needs and expectations of individuals; however, Germain states that an informal organization, such as a social organization, can provide the basic needs that the formal organization cannot provide.

Germain, like Bronfenbrenner, focuses on individuals, yet the model can be used to examine groups as well. An example of a social organization for Korean American 1.5ers is the Korean Jaycees. Within the organization, there is a set hierarchy, with established roles and procedures. However, the informal nature of the organization sets the foundation for interpersonal exchanges that foster relationships and address the intimate needs of individuals. One of the goals of the Korean Jaycees is to address the needs of the Korean community. By participating in the organization, a 1.5er not only participates in an ethnic organization, but also creates relationships with those in and outside of the organization that focus on the intimate needs of ethnic identification and formation.

Social construction theory and the identity development model are useful in examining aspects of ethnic identity. However, each on its own does not explain the process of how ethnic identities come to be. Thus, in this study I merge the theory and model to develop an alternative analysis of ethnic identity development, which I refer to as the processual experience. It is during the process of becoming 1.5 Korean American that 1.5ers experience sociocultural influences that help shape and construct this collective identity. As a result of their experiences, 1.5 Korean Americans are bicultural, bilingual, and able to switch and negotiate their ethnic options depending on the situation. Furthermore, while the sociocultural experiences contribute to the 1.5ers' characteristics, the social constructionist view also shows how in the end, 1.5ers become consciously aware of their collective 1.5 ethnic identity. The sociohistorical context becomes the major component of the ethnic identity of a particular ethnic group or subgroup. It is important to be aware that ethnic identity is not an entity, but a series of complex processes in time in which people construct from "historical" facts biographical continuities between ancestors and their descendants as a group, generally in a wider social context of other ethnic groups and other social phenomena.[31]

4

KOREAN FAMILIES
TRANSFORMED

The family has often been credited with having the most influence on an individual's socialization process. Specifically, the morals, values, and traditions that one learns from the family become embedded as part of one's identity. Although the family as an agent of socialization makes a strong impression on one's sense of self, literature on the family often overlooks the significance of the family's role in shaping their children's ethnic identity.

The family plays a crucial role in shaping Korean American children's 1.5 ethnic identity. The family, during their period of acculturating to dominant local/American culture, influences how 1.5ers navigate between being Korean and being Korean American. The 1.5ers learn the values, practices, and norms of being Korean based on the relationships they have with their parents and other family members. However, the family also influences 1.5ers' Korean and Korean American ethnic identity through discussion or lack of discussion regarding the future of the family lineage, the amount of Korean and English language spoken at home, the types of friends parents have, and the amount of interaction that the family and children have with extended family members. The amount of interaction 1.5ers have with their parents is greatly affected by whether both parents work.

Although traditional families are merely a recollection of how Korean families were at one time in Korea's long history, the foundation and much of how Korean Americans base their family functions and roles stem from this tradition.

It is difficult to discuss immigrant Korean families without examining the influence of Confucianism. Historically, Chinese cultural influences spread southward to Korea and then to Japan; thus, Chinese culture has had a greater impact on Korea than Japanese culture.[1] According to Confucian ideology, parents and children have a mutual attitude of benevolence; however, there is a one-sided obedience of the child to the parents. Moreover, the child is expected to care and provide for the parents in their older years, and even after their death must pay respect and homage to them. As for the husband–wife relationship, it is based on patriarchy. The husband is considered the provider and decision maker in the household, and the wife is expected to care for her husband, children, in-laws, and the home. Women do not have a say in decision making; in fact, the sons will in the end have more say in the welfare of the family. The old Korean saying "The bone is of the father and the flesh is of the mother" highlights how patriarchy has sustained itself over time. Age hierarchy is also significant under Confucianism

The emphasis on respecting elders is significant for sibling relationships. Because there is an understanding that age equates with authority, sibling rivalry is infrequent in Korean families.[2] Moreover, age is important in general relationships to the extent that such beliefs are manifested in honorific language to elders as well as in overall social interaction. Traditionally in Korean families, sons are valued more than daughters, and the expectations for each child are different.[3] Whereas a daughter marries and lives with her husband's family, a son continues to live with his parents. When the son marries, his wife joins him and his parents, creating an extended family.[4] Finally, the family emphasizes the importance of education. The belief that education is the gateway to social mobility and prestige is emphasized in Korean families. Through educational attainment, the parents can rest assured that their children will obtain jobs that will not only support themselves but the parents as well. Although "traditional" Confucianism has been modified, the foundation remains in Korean culture.

For Korean Americans, an immigrant Korean family is also defined as a family that speaks primarily Korean at home, eats Korean food, celebrates Korean holidays, participates in Korean organizations, has predominantly Korean friends, and enforces the values of filial piety.

Once Koreans immigrated to the United States, there were problems with fulfilling duties of filial piety. Immigration weakened the patrilineally extended family system and strengthened bilateral kinship relationships.[5] The many necessities of American life pull Korean American parents away from the home, resulting in less time being spent in the kind of purposeful cooperative activities that nurture child development.[6] Kim and Hurh (1993) state that Korean immigrants adapted to American society by combining the traditional family system with the industrial way of life in the United States into what they refer to as the extended conjugal family. They suggest that by restructuring their belief system, families develop a maturational perspective firmly rooted in the changing reality of Korean immigrants in the United States. Kim, Kim, and Hurh (1991) suggest that a revised expectation of filial piety retains the cultural norms, but a modification of it allows intergenerational relationships in Korean immigrant families to adapt to their current life conditions. Although first-generation Korean families modify the notion of family to adapt to American culture, they hold a romanticized view of how a family should be. Intellectually, first-generation families understand the need to adapt; however, they still expect their children to uphold the traditions and values of the Korean family.

Korean American families in Hawai'i are quite different from families in Korea, not because Korean Americans are "Americanized" or because they live in Hawai'i, but because their understanding and expression of what it means to be a Korean family stem from their experiences in Korea. As with any other culture, the meaning of family and what it entails constantly changes. However, being Korean American for 1.5ers is based on their memories and their parents' emphasis on what it means to be Korean. Koreanness, therefore, is based on the information gathered from parents, Korean friends, and Korean media and may not be how Koreans in Korea define or express Koreanness. Once Korean families come to Hawai'i, they are no longer "Korean families." Instead, these immigrant families become Korean American families, and a newly constructed expression and meaning of family emerges. Hence, the immigrant families along with the 1.5ers and subsequent generations of Korean Americans themselves continually reconstruct and re-create what it means to be a Korean American family.

The Korean American families in this study immigrated to Hawai'i from the early 1970s to the mid-1980s; thus their "Koreanness" is based on expressions of being "Korean" during that time period. As one subject stated, the parents of 1.5ers are in a time capsule; their understanding and expression of being a Korean family is based on their experiences from the past and is not necessarily representative of what it means to be a family today in Korea. As a result, families may hold on to more "traditional" Korean cultural values and in many ways glorify these cultural traits and traditions to their children.

As mentioned earlier, Korean immigrant families experience a different set of roles, activities, and interpersonal relationships in the United States than families in Korea. Women, in particular, experience higher status in their homes; 56 percent of Korean American women contribute to the family income.[7] Although their status at home has improved, they have the added burden of a second shift at home after putting in a full day's work. What the literature fails to note is that the 1.5 generation children are also given "jobs" in the home—as interpreters, mail sorters and readers, financiers, and overall surrogate household heads and caregivers to younger siblings. Thus, while memories of the roles and functions of the traditional Korean family remain, added to the family structure is the creation of Korean American values, norms, and practices.

For aging parents, the changing family structure creates various problems. Korean parents come to the United States with hopes of a better life for their children, only to find that they must depend on their children for basic functions that they took for granted in Korea. Due in part to their lack of English proficiency, parents find themselves asking for advice and suggestions from their children, contrary to the Confucian ideology of age equating with wisdom. In addition, parents begin to justify their children's non-Korean attitudes and behaviors as the result of American influences and begin to modify their notion of filial piety. Grandparents who come to live with their first-generation child and family quickly realize that their roles now include taking care of the grandchildren and keeping house while their married child is at work.[8] In some cases, grandparents feel slighted, neglected, and humiliated in their child's home. In a new country away from their familiar surroundings, grandparents are unable to speak the language, do not receive attention or care from their children, and feel as if they have no advice to offer them. Some grandparents feel marginalized in their child's home and seek independence by moving into government-subsidized senior citizen apartments.[9] Immigration itself creates a new set of social and cultural conditions under which the fabric of the Korean American family is transformed.

The shift from the extended to the nuclear family also affects gender roles in the Korean American family. Changes in the mother's role resocialize 1.5 and second-generation children into new gender roles. Unlike their parents, who were raised with the notion of filial piety, the children view their mother's role as a working mom rather than as a housewife. However, in working-class families, the children see the mother's job as an economic necessity and in many ways pity their mom for having to work, for example, as a maid. This encourages some to better their lives so as not to recycle the economic conditions in their home. As a result of both parents working, children are more likely to view an egalitarian partnership between parents as the family norm. Additionally, the idea of grandparents living with them under the same roof becomes a foreign concept as more grandparents opt to live in their own apartments rather than be the "housemaids" for their children and grandchildren.

The 1.5 generation children may also experience generational conflicts with their parents. Although there are parent–child conflicts in all American families, the conflicts are more serious in Korean American families due to the language barrier and value differences. The 1.5ers speak only conversational Korean, whereas most Korean parents have difficulty speaking English well. For second-generation children, the language barrier is more intense. Therefore, often in Korean American families, the parents speak Korean and the children speak Korean, English, and/or Konglish to each other and to their parents.

In addition to the language barrier between first-generation parents and their children, Korean parents embrace traditional values of hard work, family ties, social status, education, and other standards that they fear are unimportant to their children. The generational conflicts create distance between Korean parents and their children.[10] Korean American 1.5ers, during this part of the process, appear not to appreciate the Korean values prescribed by their parents. However, these Korean values influence their sense of being Korean, and later in the process they find that this aspect of their socialization contributes to their ethnic identity as 1.5ers.

In light of structural constraints and cultural limitations, Korean Americans have had to adopt a variety of survival strategies that have resulted in variations in family life. These family variations are the product of social and economic conditions with which Korean Americans have been forced to cope.[11] In order to adapt to the American way of life, the 1.5 generation find themselves in between two cultures, having to reconstruct a Korean American family that includes both first and second generations and Korean, local, and American cultures. Much of the family modification results from how the notion of family is socially constructed through the combined influences of immigrant families, television and other media, and friends' parents.

Memories of Korea and exposure to Korean values and culture contribute to 1.5ers' identification with being Korean during this part of the process. Under the conditions of family influence, 1.5ers learn how to express their Koreanness through language, cultural nuances, and social interactions with other Korean Americans. Yet they also learn to construct an alternative ethnicity as Korean American and learn from their experiences at home what it means to be Korean American.

Social Construction of Family

As first-generation parents strive to develop a sense of home in a new country, 1.5ers and their parents simultaneously construct what it means to be a family in the United States. Like all parents, immigrant parents develop a sense of family function and structure early on from their own experience with their parents. The challenge for first-generation parents is that their frame of reference for what is a family is based on their experiences in Korea. They may attempt to pass on the notion of filial piety and other Confucian beliefs, but the social and structural reinforcement is lacking in Hawai'i. Korean families are not able to practice and fully enforce Korean values and beliefs with their 1.5 and second-generation children due to social, cultural, and economic complications. The changes faced by both parents and children help to construct what it means to be a Korean American family.

The 1.5ers are socialized at home and thus learn aspects of Korean culture and values from their parents, which affect their identification with being Korean. However, what they learn at home is often contrary to what they observe in other families around them. Television and non-Korean families provide models of what a mother and father should be like, how parents and children should interact, and how siblings should get along. The media portrays an image of a family that contradicts 1.5ers' observations in their own home. Prominent television shows with family themes such as *Leave It to Beaver* in the 1950s and 1960s, *The Brady Bunch* in the 1970s, *Eight Is Enough* in the 1980s, *Cosby* in the mid-1980s, and *Home Improvement* in the 1990s portray an American family in which communication is central—whether it be communication between parents, between parents and children, or between siblings. American television attempts to portray a family that is fairly egalitarian and in which the children have the right to express themselves and disagree with their parents. Regardless of the issue, at the end of the 30 minutes, conflicts and tensions have been resolved through talking with parents.

Such portrayals affect how 1.5ers see their own families. Luann, a 32-year-old social worker, says of her father, "He doesn't acknowledge good things. Doesn't say, 'I'm proud of you,' but points to the negative." Robert, a 35-year-old lawyer, says,

*My dad did not show any emotion; he never said
he loved us or praised us. I never felt like I did
well enough, because he had no problems telling
us when we didn't do something right. His thinking is, nothing said is nothing bad; why should I
have to say anything? You should know. His love
was understood, his devotion was understood,
and everything is understood without saying.
There was never any sign of physical love or ver-
bal. The only times he said anything was in writing. Like in a card, he said I love you and I'm
proud of you, but never in person. My mom is
not affectionate either, but she always lets you
know what's on her mind. Sometimes she says
stuff without thinking, but that's a reason why
she's so happy. She never holds things in. Unlike
my dad, who holds everything in. He doesn't like
to tell anyone his problems; he thinks he can handle it on his own.*

The presentation of families in the media contradicts
the immediate experience of the 1.5ers in their homes.
Such observations affect how 1.5ers view their family and
behave at home. Although 1.5ers play an active role in
maintaining the family by paying the bills, acting as interpreters, and managing the overall functions of the family,
their experience at home is neither traditionally Korean
nor American but rather Korean American. Thus,
through a combination of family and media they begin to
construct a Korean American identity and family.

The families of Korean American 1.5ers' friends reinforce television images of the family. As 1.5ers start
school and develop friendships, they have more exposure
to other households. Observations of peers' families reaffirm that the 1.5er's family is different from others in
Hawai'i. The friends do not handle the overall family
functions, nor do they translate for their parents. Thus,
1.5ers base their model of a family on three frames of

reference: their own family, friends' families, and the media. Hence, the 1.5er's family is a product of the family's adaptation to American and Korean family functions.

Community and Its Impact on Family Life

In 1990 43.4 percent of Korean Americans lived in the west, and the rest were scattered through the United States.[12] Los Angeles has the largest concentration of Koreans, followed by New York and Chicago. With the exception of Koreatown in Los Angeles, Koreans are geographically dispersed throughout metropolitan areas. Although first-generation Korean immigrants tend to work in predominantly Korean American neighborhoods, they show the highest level of suburban residency among ethnic groups in suburban areas.[13] The suburbs provide good schools and a "safe environment," contributing to 1.5 and second-generation Korean Americans' remarkable achievements in schoolwork. In New York, two Korean Americans have received the Presidential Scholars Award, which is given to the two best high school seniors in each state.[14] The suburban community's good school systems not only help produce exceptional students but also help reinforce Korean parents' emphasis on education.[15] Although Korean Americans generally live in the suburbs, Hurh and Kim (1984b) found that first-generation Korean Americans had predominantly Korean friends and neighbors. Moreover, 90 percent of Korean Americans are affiliated with one or more Korean organizations. Korean Americans who socialize or work primarily with Koreans may find little need to speak English, particularly when business transactions, social activities, and community functions are conducted within the Korean community.

A community that is ethnically organized can be supportive to the families and individuals within it. For example, the 1990 New York boycott of two Korean merchants brought community organizations and members together to keep the two stores open. The support of the Korean American community revealed how much influence it has on the people who work and live in it. An ethnic enclave can also work against Korean Americans. In 1992, during the Los Angeles riots after the Rodney King verdict, Korean American merchants and families called for police protection in fear of angry mobs attacking their stores and homes. The police, however, were off protecting the residents of Beverly Hills while Korean Americans were fending off looters and watching the demise of their businesses and homes.[16] The Korean merchants in Los Angeles were situated in an area known for its interethnic conflicts and lower-income residents, and police officers in the Los Angeles area opted to protect the more "respected" community members.[17] Although the Korean American community can band together to support each other, the LA riot illustrated the need for structural support. Still, the primary needs and concerns of Korean communities are those of the first generation, which helps to push the 1.5 and second generations from the Korean community.

In Hawai'i 1.5ers express similar sentiments of marginality in the Korean American community. Because of the community being led by first-generation immigrants, 1.5ers believe that when as adults they begin to participate in community affairs, they are not taken seriously and are seen merely as "children" of the leaders in the community. Mark, a 25-year-old 1.5er, states,

> We as 1.5s can understand the needs of the Korean community, but at the same time understand how to deal with the American culture. Our method of communicating with non-Koreans is more likely to bridge the relationship with the [Korean] community and the others [non-Korean community]. But the first generation

*still will not let go of the control and still treat us
like children*

As a result of the first generation's Confucian belief system, the elders consider themselves the wise decision makers, with the younger generations there to learn from their wisdom and experience. However, as Mark explains, it is difficult to conduct business the Korean way, and there is a need to begin exploring business dealings beyond just Koreans. As a result of the first generation infantilizing the 1.5ers, some 1.5ers have a tendency to avoid social relationships with them. John, a 25-year-old 1.5er, explains, "With my job, there are times that I have to work with first-generation Koreans, but it is not my choice. I end up with them because of my [Korean] speaking abilities."

A majority of Korean American parents work in small businesses as proprietors or managers, often working long hours under stressful conditions.[18] Particularly in the Los Angeles area, local merchants are faced with the constant potential of interethnic conflict with other minority groups in urban neighborhoods. With the daily pressures of work and the understandable fear of violence, parents may not be as inclined to participate in a nurturing, responsive, and reciprocal manner in the family microsystem.[19] Furthermore, the perceived danger from the African American community perpetuates negative stereotypes. Parents may be resistant to their children dating or socializing with African Americans. This may in turn affect the way children view African Americans in their community.

Korean American families with their own businesses, often with both parents working, put in long hours 6 to 7 days a week.[20] Forty-six percent of Korean American elementary and high school students interviewed in New York stated that there is no one at home when they return from school.[21] In extended families, grandparents may serve as the caregivers, yet not all first-generation families have grandparents living with them. For these families, unsupervised children who are not interested in studying may go out, meet friends, and possibly get caught up in delinquent behavior.[22] In Hawai'i, although there are a number of small Korean businesses, dual-income families are prevalent among the working class. Children of these families are often left to fend for themselves after school and care for their younger siblings. Mark, a 27-year-old, remembers picking up his sister when he was only 9 years old. He says,

> *My parents worried a lot when I was in third grade. We lived on Wilder Street back then. My sister would be with the babysitter, so I'd go to the sitter's house and pick up my sis and take her back home; it was just a block away. Back then it was a lot safer and the sitter could literally see us walking from her house to ours. One time, my mom went to the sitter's house to find out that I had picked up my sister from the house; from there, I guess she gained trust in me 'cause I just started doing that. It's weird to think now, a third grader doing that. But I was alone at home and I just thought to pick her up.*

Families and Education

With a strong emphasis on Confucian ideology, Korean Americans have great respect for educated people and therefore emphasize the importance of education to their children.[23] Koreans believe education is the main avenue for social mobility. In Korea, parents spend a large amount of money on private tutors, extracurricular activities, and exam preparation courses for their children. Korean American parents consider their child's education and their own careers as equally important.[24] Landon, a 25-year-old 1.5er, recalls,

When I was in intermediate high school our family was really poor. I mean, we didn't have a car, we were on welfare, and the five of us lived in a two-bedroom apartment. My dad is and was then a taxi driver, and my mom worked as a housekeeper in a hotel. Still, my parents put all the money together so I could go to a private school; they wanted me to have the same types of opportunities as other, rich kids.

Children of first-generation parents face various strains in regard to education. They are aware of how important education is to their parents and feel a lot of pressure to succeed in school. Although many students succeed in school, others are not as successful. Due to language barriers, cultural differences, feelings of alienation, and discrimination at school, an unsuccessful Korean American student may be inclined to participate in delinquent acts. Young, a 22-year-old 1.5er, explains:

In Hawai'i, there are so many 1.5s who drop out of school. I see them entering college, but then drop out after a semester or a year. They don't do well in school so they drop out. A lot of them end up working in restaurants, hotel, or retail and then go out and spend it. They go out almost every night to clubs, drinking and some take drugs. I see so many 1.5s in trouble, not all of them are successful. Many are in trouble . . . some are in gangs.

Problems at school and little to no supervision at home lead some into delinquent activities. For some families, involvement in gangs produces a whole new set of rules and behaviors, which makes relationships at home difficult. Korean Americans in Hawai'i during the 1980s had a significant problem with gangs. One first-generation Korean historian states,

We had a bad problem with Korean gangs. Young men who would get together threatened

businesses for protection money. Some would follow the bar hostesses and rob them; a large proportion of them sold [ice].

[The Korean community] got together with the help of the YMCA and created an outlet for the youths, so they had a place to go. It was quite successful and we saw less kids on the streets and in gangs. We no longer hear about the gang problems now.

Intra-/Interracial Dating and Courtship

Korean immigrant parents are concerned with maintaining the family lineage and the Korean American community into future generations. They want their children to marry Koreans; in fact, some parents go as far as to recruit potential spouses from Korea for their children to make sure they remain within the ethnic fold and inherit family and community.[25] One reason Korean American parents have felt compelled to turn to Korea to recruit spouses for their children is the lack here of Korean men and women for them, and Koreans in Korea saw that marrying a Korean American represented a good social and economic opportunity for them.[26] However, it has become more difficult to recruit spouses from Korea due to its growing economy. Koreans no longer see Korean Americans as a good catch but rather as an idle choice.

Korean American 1.5ers who are of marrying age experience conflicts with Korean values concerning marriage. Kitano and colleagues (1984) refer to the 1.5ers as the "knee-high" generation in which the women have acculturated more rapidly and adapted more quickly to the new American culture than their male counterparts. The women have learned English, adapted to Hawaiian and American ways, changed their names to American ones, and dressed in American fashions. However, their parents have continued to reinforce the traditional Korean family structure in which the male members, especially the firstborn son, enjoy elevated status and authority roles. For 1.5 Korean American women, the egalitarian American family system is more desirable, and the search for equality leads to a search for relationships outside the traditional Korean culture. Thus, the prevailing family system in which the 1.5er grew up will most likely affect his or her attitude toward dating Koreans.

In Hawai'i, both 1.5 generation women and men express a preference toward marry non-Koreans, but they also state that a second-generation Korean American may be acceptable. The reason the women cite is that Korean American men are chauvinistic and conservative; the men maintain that Korean American women are materialistic and judgmental. Even though the women find the traditional patriarchal relationship undesirable, they still prize the Confucian values of education and family. Joanne, a 25-year-old female 1.5er, states, "I would never marry a Korean man. They are just too Korean, you know . . . too conservative, too sexist, too . . . expecting [women] to do all the housework and stuff like that." When asked about her most recent relationship with a non-Korean male, she replied,

> *Well, the reason why we broke up is because he is not goal oriented. You know, he's in college and everything, but he just doesn't know what he wants to do with his life. He doesn't have a goal. He is OK with just hanging out with his friends drinking beer and watching TV, but I need someone who is going to make something of himself.*

Although this sentiment may not be exclusive to Korean 1.5ers, such goal orientation is often what first-generation parents cite as a prerequisite in a partner for their daughter. As for males, although they express a distaste for the materialism and assertiveness often equated with Westernization, they also state that they would like a "nice girl." Dan, a 26-year-old 1.5er, states,

For me, the woman I will ultimately marry has to be a "nice girl." I don't want someone who's going to party all the time, I like a girl who is more old-fashioned. . . . When I get married, I prefer that my wife stay home and not work. Taking care of the house and kids is already a lot of work.

Both Joanne and Dan say that they do not wish to date or marry a Korean, but they seek mates with Korean-type characteristics. Although this seems contradictory on the surface, their preference is linked to their feelings of being in between two cultures. They reject certain Korean attributes, but they also seek someone with Korean values and beliefs. Ron, a 30-year-old, states, "What I'm looking for is someone like me. Someone with ties in Hawai'i, Korea, and the United States. I think it's important to have someone who understands my culture, which is a combination of all three."

Korean American 1.5ers in an intra-ethnic relationship face less resistance from their parents but report more stress from having the whole family involved in the relationship. Hilary, a 23-year-old 1.5er, states, "When you are in a relationship with another Korean, it is pretty interesting. You know the relationship is no longer with just you and your boyfriend, but your family and their family get involved. There's a lot of pressure to marry when you are dating a Korean."

Kitano and colleagues (1984) report that more Korean American women than men marry out, and that this is partially due to the new role of women in the United States, with men still treated by first-generation parents under the Confucian ideology. They found that in Hawai'i, there is a high level of out-marriage. According to the authors, Korean Americans who live in a more racially tolerant community are likely to marry outside their ethnic group. What is interesting to note is that the Korean out-marriage rate in Hawai'i is the highest among all ethnic groups, whereas in Los Angeles it is the lowest. Although the idea of a more racially tolerant community may be a factor in the number of interracial marriages, Hawai'i also has a larger percentage of Korean women married to military personnel. In addition, Korean Americans in Hawai'i have had the longest residency in the United States compared with those elsewhere, leading to a greater chance of intermarriage.

John, a 26-year-old 1.5er who is in a relationship with a Caucasian-Korean woman, states, "It's great being in a relationship with [her]. Since her mom is Korean, she understands Korean culture and values, she eats Korean food, and can understand Korean a little. Still, she is also half white, so she isn't so Korean, if you know what I mean."

Divorce

Along with the higher rates of intermarriage among Korean Americans in Hawai'i and the United States, there has also been an increase in divorce. Min (1995) gives three reasons for this. First, as a result of extended residency in the United States, Korean Americans' attitudes toward divorce have changed from it being deviant to being socially acceptable. Second, Korean Americans who find partners in Korea marry after a month or two of courtship, which leaves little time for them to get to know each other's personal and family backgrounds. And third, Korean War brides are associated with high divorce rates. Min asserts that even with a growing number of Korean Americans divorcing, their families are still more "stable" than white American families.

The notion of stability is as fluid as people's attitude toward divorce. As with many things, attitudes about relationships are influenced by social, political, and cultural factors that affect everyday interactions. Although the three reasons proposed by Min are viable, they are merely explanations for divorce in the mid-1970s to late

1980s. Among 1.5 and second-generation Korean Americans, there is less intermarriage between Korean American women and U.S. military personnel but an increasing number of interracial marriages.

Although statistics in the past have cited higher divorce rates among interracial marriages,[27] there has also been a growing number of intraracial divorces. Two major factors explain the recent shift in the divorce rate between Korean Americans. First, first-generation women who in Korea did not work but relied solely on their husbands for economic support, find that in the United States they contribute equally and sometimes more to the household income. They are no longer financially dependent on their spouses and shoulder much of the economic responsibility, leading to a new sense of independence that is contrary to the "traditional" Korean woman's role. Second, 1.5 generation Korean Americans carry both American and Korean cultural values and beliefs, which often contradict each other. As a result, they may seek and marry a partner with Korean values that conflict with their Westernized views about marriage. Lynn, a 31-year-old 1.5er divorcee, states,

> *I married my ex-husband because he was everything that my ex-boyfriend was not. He was attentive, loving, and wanted to be with me all the time. But after a while, it got too much. He was too possessive and controlling and wanted to be with me all the time. What I fell in love with to begin with turned out to be the reason why I divorced.*

David, a 26-year-old 1.5er, speaks about his father's past three marriages with Korean women. David states that regardless of what may happen, he knows that his father will be married because he is in love with love, even if the relationship may not be right for him. He states, "Dad just can't let go [of being married]. He has such poor choice of women. With his current wife, they fight and yell and say that they're going to get divorced. I tell him, get divorced already."[28]

Changes in the Korean American Family

The change in family structure may prove to be particularly confusing for American-raised (1.5 generation) and American-born (second generation) children. They may initially feel marginalized between the two cultures by trying to reconstruct their identity to fit both American and Korean ethnicities. Although first-, 1.5, and second-generation Korean Americans may experience an extended conjugal family system, it is unclear what type of family will emerge for the third, fourth, and subsequent Korean American generations. As more Korean women intermarry, our understanding of the Korean American family is apt to change.[29] Moreover, the intercultural influence of a biracial couple is also likely to affect the child's identity and the family dynamics.

Another factor that may alter how we view the Korean American family are the laws on domestic partnership. Although little has been said about same-sex relationships among Korean Americans specifically and Asian Americans generally, a growing number of Asian American homosexuals are coming out to their families. For Korean American families, such "outings" can affect the whole filial system, which is still to some extent ingrained in the family. Mike, a 26-year-old 1.5er gay male, talks about the problems he had with coming out to his mom and to his immediate and extended family. He says,

> I came out to my mom when we were arguing. I know it wasn't the best scenario, but she got me so mad that I guess I came out to hurt her even more. I just shouted out "I'm gay!" Surprisingly, she was pretty cool about it. She asked me if I was sure and then she just seemed to accept it. The thing is, though, she came out for me to my brother and sister, which I didn't really appreciate. To this day I don't talk to them about my sexuality. We just don't talk about it.

When asked about his mother's calm demeanor, Mike replied, "I think it was easier because I'm not the only son. I mean if I was the only son, then who would carry on the family name? (Laughs.) I would like to have a child someday, but I would have to adopt, of course, and it wouldn't be my blood. You know how Koreans are about it being their blood."

For families with gay children, filial piety is modified and reconstructed to fit the needs of both parents and children. Moreover, as more gay Korean Americans partake in domestic partnership, the whole concept of what it means to be a Korean American family in the United States must be reexamined.

The future of Korean American families lies heavily on the 1.5 generation. Whether the emphasis in the family is Korean, American, or an adaptation of the two cultures rests in the hands of the future generation. What is clear, however, is that among the 1.5 there is a growing interest in Korean American ethnic identity.

The 1.5 generation Korean Americans are tomorrow's parents and leaders of their community. They will help create what a Korean American family is. With a decline in the number of professional immigrants and a proportionate increase in working-class Koreans, the professional community is left under the auspices of the 1.5 generation Korean Americans. The transferring of family traditions, values, and beliefs will be left to this generation, and through them, there will emerge a new Korean American family.

5

SOCIAL CLASS, FAMILY, AND ETHNIC IDENTITY

Social Class and Korean American Families

The lingering stereotype of Korean American families is that they are all wealthy, own their own businesses, and pressure their children to go to Harvard University. The reality is that Korean Americans come from different socioeconomic, political, and religious backgrounds and have varying cultural customs and dialects. Social class can greatly affect the function and lifestyle of Korean American families and consequently affect the way children in the families construct their ethnic identity. The social class of the family provides opportunities and a basis for family life, including the neighborhood where one resides, the schools the 1.5ers attend, and the social interactions that are available for both first-generation parents and 1.5 children. Although there are obviously more than two social classes, for the purpose of this study, I differentiate between "middle-class" and "working-class" Korean American families.

The question of what categorizes a family as working class or middle class seems straightforward enough. The U.S. Census distinguishes incomes and occupations among ethnic groups, which can be used as a marker for class. However, there are some problems with using this simple formula for determining the social class of Korean American families. A discussion on social class is a book in itself, and is not the purpose or the intent of this chapter. What is central to the discussion of class is whether there is a shared class consciousness. Although families may meet the minimum income level to be considered "middle class," they may not feel middle class. Thus, the feeling or the consciousness of being a member of a particular social class extends beyond income and encompasses history and experience. A simplistic formula equating income with social class dismisses the history of Korean American families prior to their income earning in the United States. For example, when professional Koreans immigrated to the United States, they found their degrees and education useless without the ability to speak English. Korean Americans who held middle-class positions in Korea found that in Hawai'i their education and credentials did not matter in competing for positions with Koreans who held significantly lower-paying jobs in Korea. Some of the professionals thus turned to more "working-class" occupations while making "middle-class" earnings. An example of this group are the taxi drivers who freelance and "float" for companies that cater predominantly to a Korean American clientele. Taxi driving is not a prestigious occupation but can bring in the income to purchase a home in Hawai'i and send children to private schools. At the same time, this occupation allows some to manipulate the system by not documenting all their earnings and thus appearing to bring in "working-class" wages. Economically, first-generation Korean Americans are able to achieve new social class standing and may be able to obtain financial security that they could not in Korea.

Regardless of their earning potential, working-class Korean Americans continue to fight for social equity. Although they may be able to present themselves and live as middle class, their consciousness and their social acceptance and recognition by others continue to distinguish them as working class. Thus, I conceptualize middle-class families as those that have at least one parent with a high school degree or higher and who held a professional or non–labor-intensive job in Korea. Working-class families are those where both parents have less than a high school education and worked in the service or labor market in Korea. The significance of studying the effects of the family on Korean American 1.5 ethnic identity is twofold. By examining the disparate social class status of Korean American families in Hawai'i, we can begin to decipher the role of socioeconomic status on the process of becoming a 1.5er, that is, whether the social class of the family influences how 1.5ers construct their Koreanness and Korean Americanness.

Social class usually determines the neighborhood where a family resides, the schools the children attend, and the community and social outlets to which the parents expose their children. All of this contributes to how 1.5ers see themselves as Korean American in Hawai'i. Whether a family chooses to live in predominantly Korean, local, or white neighborhoods will ultimately influence how their children view their ethnicity, culture, and family.

Case Studies of 1.5ers and Their Working-Class Families

The 1.5ers from working-class families identify themselves as feeling in between the first and second generations, or as 1.5 Korean American, and are bilingual, bicultural, and able to switch ethnic identities. The following three case studies help illustrate how working-class families influence 1.5ers' construction of Korean and Korean American ethnic identities. In this chapter, the case studies will be used to illustrate the family's influence in maintaining a Korean ethnic identity and in transforming and constructing a Korean American identity in the children's process of becoming 1.5ers.

I first give a brief background of the case studies and then examine how the family influences 1.5ers' sense of being Korean—specifically, how 1.5ers' memories of their early immigrant experience and neighborhood and their parents' friends influence their identification with being Korean. Then I examine how the family affects 1.5ers' transformation and construction of Korean American ethnic identity—specifically, how language and parent–child relationships influence 1.5ers' identification with being Korean American.

Jenny Lee

Jenny Lee, a 24-year-old, immigrated in 1982, when she was 7 years old, with her mother, 10-year-old sister, and 2-year-old brother. Her father was already working as a fisherman in Hawai'i and brought them over when he had enough money saved. Mr. Lee dropped out of high school to work on a fishing boat in Korea, and Mrs. Lee finished third grade and worked odd jobs until they married. Her father's job required him to be away from home a lot. Her mother had a difficult time raising three children by herself, so the family decided that the eldest, Jane, would live with her paternal grandmother while Jenny and James lived with their mom. Jenny says that she saw her sister Jane about twice a year, and they were reunited when they met at Seoul Airport to leave for Hawai'i.

Jenny attended public schools all her life and did not foster close relationships with Korean Americans; instead, her friends were largely other 1.5 Asian Americans. Jenny wanted to attend a university in the continental United States, but due to a family emergency stayed in Hawai'i to attend college. Jenny graduated from college in 1997 and works as an assistant manager at a wholesale company. She currently lives with her parents and brother but hopes to move to the States in the next few years.

ANDY SHIM

Andy, a 29-year-old, immigrated to Hawai'i with his parents and brother in 1973, when he was 5 years old. The Shim family was sponsored by their mother's sister, who was married to a Caucasian man, who convinced the whole family to immigrate. All of Andy's family members on his mother's side immigrated to Hawai'i. Mr. Shim finished third grade and joined the service, and Mrs. Shim finished second grade and was a housewife in Korea. Today, his father works at an auto body shop and his mom until about 5 years ago worked for a manufacturer.

Andy attended public elementary school early on, but later attended St. Patrick private school and St. Louis High School. In school, he had primarily local friends. His four best friends are Filipino, Hawaiian-Japanese, Vietnamese, and Chinese. He never had any Korean American friends growing up, largely because there were few of them when he was in school. After graduating from high school he attended college in Hawai'i and went to the States for graduate school. Andy received his master's degree and now works as a computer analyst in Honolulu. In the States, he met his fiancée, a local girl from Hawai'i. Up until the spring of 1998, Andy was living with his parents and brother in East Honolulu, but recently he purchased a condominium close to his parents.

DAN KIM

Dan, a 26-year-old, immigrated to Hawai'i in 1980, when he was 8 years old, with his father. His parents separated when he was 5 years old for reasons unknown to him; he never asked his father for an explanation. His paternal aunts raised him while his dad worked as a machinist in Saudi Arabia. When Dan was 7, his dad began dating a woman who soon moved to Hawai'i. Before he knew it, he and his dad joined her in Hawai'i. Dan did not find out until later that his dad had married this woman, Ann, in

Korea. Her sister, who was married to an American ser-
viceman in Hawai'i, later sponsored Dan, and his dad
sponsored Ann.

Dan attended public schools all his life. Growing up he
befriended local boys in his neighborhood and did not
have close relationships with Korean Americans. After
Dan graduated from high school, he decided to go to the
States to attend a machinist school, which he did for 2 years
but decided not to finish. He returned to Hawai'i and
began work in the tourist industry. Throughout his adult
life, he lived with his father and stepmothers but lived on
his own for a year. Dan currently works in the tourist industry and his father works for a Korean-owned taxi
company. Since their immigration to Hawai'i, his father
has divorced Ann and married another Korean woman
but is currently in the process of getting a divorce.

Memories of Being an Immigrant

Korean identity is maintained largely by 1.5ers' memories
of Korea and/or their immigrant experience in Hawai'i.
Korean American 1.5ers remember not understanding
English, and feeling frustrated and alienated because they
could not understand a word of what was said to them.
The "culture shock" of entering a new country and feeling alienated is an experience that is shared by 1.5ers. The
feeling of not belonging remains with them and reinforces
their identification with being Korean and not "American"
or local in the early part of the process of becoming a 1.5er.
Although 1.5ers have memories of living in Korea, their
memories of Korea take the form of snapshot images.
Especially for those who came when they were young,
they recall the feelings and experiences they had as children more than having clear memories of Korea as a
country. For those who attended elementary school in
Korea, their memories of Korean schools include having
to take their shoes off; eating *kimchee*, rice, and fish for

lunch; and receiving or observing physical punishment by teachers. But regardless of their age at the time of immigration, 1.5ers remember wanting to immigrate to "America," a place where food is in abundance and success achievable.

Although memories of Korea are scattered, 1.5ers clearly remember their experiences as immigrants in Hawai'i. One memory that stands out for many 1.5ers is being picked on or ridiculed for their differences. Other kids and adults alike made fun of their accents, the way they dressed, and their inability to understand English or pidgin. Korean American 1.5ers recall not understanding English. Andy said, "Initially I felt alienated because I could not speak English. We heard people say 'go back to your country.'" Jenny recalls being picked on because of her Korean accent and "FOBBY" dress, and Dan remembers having to reenter the third grade because he could not speak a word of English. These early images had two effects on the 1.5ers. First, it reinforced to them that they were strangers in a new land, separating them from others. Regardless of how much they wanted to fit in to the larger Hawai'i society, those around them reminded them of their Koreanness. Thus, in this part of the process they claimed their Korean identity, not by choice but by default. While they struggled to assimilate to the larger society, others still saw them as Korean immigrants. Second, although they identified as Korean in this part of the process, such negative memories of their early experience affected how 1.5ers wanted to appear to non-Koreans in Hawai'i. In this early part of their process of becoming 1.5, they learned that being an immigrant was something to avoid if one wanted to fit in with the rest of society. Yet in this part of the process it was difficult to abandon their Korean identity even if they wanted to, largely because of their parents. The parents' choices in friends and neighborhood contributed to whom the 1.5ers were exposed to on a daily basis.

Neighborhood and Friends

The neighborhood in which families live determines the ethnic composition of neighbors, whom the parents and children befriend, and the schools that the children attend. For working-class parents, the choice of neighborhood varies, yet how 1.5ers feel about being Korean is affected by where they live and whom they interact with in the neighborhood.

Jenny's family rented houses and apartments in various areas of Honolulu but currently live in public housing. They initially lived with the father's friend in Kailua before they moved into town. They remained in town because it was easier on the mother, who never learned how to drive and relied on the bus to take her to and from work. Moreover, with the father gone most of the year, it was easier for her mother to find Korean friends in town. If they were to live in the suburbs or in the country, Mrs. Lee would feel isolated due to the language barrier and her inability to drive to town. Although Jenny's parents earn enough to purchase a home, the family's official income qualifies them for public housing and allows her parents to save money.

Their residence makes it easier for Mrs. Lee to maintain relationships with other Korean American women who live in the same housing area. After she gets off work as a housekeeper, Mrs. Lee is on the phone with her Korean neighbors discussing their jobs, family, and friends. In addition, Mrs. Lee's friends and their children regularly drop by for lunch or dinner or just to watch television. This environment helps Mrs. Lee feel a part of the community, having friends with whom she can confide and who help create a sense of place for her. Furthermore, the daily interaction between Mrs. Lee and her first-generation friends gives an opportunity for Jenny to interact with other Korean Americans. With no extended family in Hawai'i, the friendships that her mother fostered become a calabash extended family of sorts.

The Lee family residence also established the children's school district. Although the Lee family had the opportunity to send their children to private school, the neighborhood in which they live reinforced their decision to send their children to public schools near their home. With their friends sending their children to public schools, they did not see a significant difference in attractiveness between the two school systems. Jenny's father in particular stresses that his children get a good education. What is important to him is that his children finish high school and enter college. Although Jenny received a good education in public school, she felt that her parents could have sent her to college on the mainland so that she could have experienced a different set of culture and educational experiences.

ANDY

Andy's family lived with his aunt in Hawai'i Kai when they immigrated. After his parents found work in town, the family moved into a one-bedroom apartment close to their parents' workplaces. The location made it easier for his parents to coordinate their commute together to work. For the first 6 years, Andy's grandmother took care of him and his brother. Unlike Jenny's family, the Shims had relatives who were already established in Hawai'i. As a result, having Korean neighbors or Korean people close by was not a significant consideration in choosing their residence. Andy's exposure to other Korean Americans was through his extended family. Together the Shim families celebrated Korean New Year, Korean Thanksgiving, and birthday parties. The interactions with his extended family helped reinforce Korean culture for Andy.

In addition, the parents learned from their relatives about the desirable neighborhoods and schools for their children. The Shims had working-class jobs, his mom in a manufacturing company and his dad as a machinist, but they struggled to provide the best for their children. Andy states that his parents sacrificed a lot to send him to private schools, college, and then graduate school. Andy's family now lives in a home in Hawai'i Kai, which they purchased. Although Andy had the influence of Korean ethnicity from his immediate and extended family, he did not have any Korean American friends at school.

DAN

When Dan and his dad arrived in Hawai'i, they moved into a two-bedroom apartment in town over a gun shop with his new stepmother and stepsister. They remained in town because his father worked as a taxi driver and his stepmother worked in a restaurant in town. Growing up in a blended Korean family and extended stepfamilies, Dan felt alienated from his stepfamily members. To Dan, they were not his real family, and he felt like an outsider in his own home. Dan states that what helped him the most during this period were his local neighbors and friends.

Dan's next-door neighbor had a son who attended the same public school, and they "instantly became best friends." Although in his home he had mainly Korean influences, such as having social gatherings with first-generation Koreans, speaking predominantly Korean at home, and hearing about the Korean community and its members, outside of the home he was heavily influenced by his local friends.

For the 1.5 case studies, their families contributed to their Korean ethnicity. Through their families, extended families, and family friends they were exposed to daily interactions with other first-generation Korean Americans. From their observations and interactions with other Korean Americans they formed their idea of what it means to be Korean. Sociocultural characteristics such as how to celebrate Korean holidays and how to interact with older Korean Americans were learned as a result of their early socialization with Korean Americans.

These 1.5ers, like many other Korean Americans, live in Honolulu, where their residences are closer to work. However, the urban area of Honolulu is economically stratified. There are clear boundaries delineating where each social class resides. The Lee family lives in an area that is openly marked "low-income state housing." As mentioned earlier, regardless of the "real" earned family income, they present themselves as and believe themselves to be working class. The state housing area is an interesting phenomenon in itself. The ethnic composition of the housing complex where the Lee family resides is predominantly Chinese and Korean, whereas the housing complex across the street is composed of Hawaiians, Samoans, and Filipinos. Thus, these marginalized ethnic groups are segregated into two distinct areas.

Andy's family lived in town but mostly in Hawai'i Kai, which is considered to be a middle-class area with a mixed ethnic composition of locals and haoles. There are no visible representations of Korean Americans in this area. Yet the parents' reasons for living in Hawai'i Kai have to do with what they felt was best for their children. The Shim family benefited from having an established family in Hawai'i before they immigrated, family members who pointed out the differences between neighborhoods and schools. Andy's exposure to his Korean side was consistent with the help of his extended family, but his neighborhood provided a setting for him to develop relationships with local friends.

Dan's family lived in an area where most of the residents were Locals. The neighbors in his apartment complex and nearby were working-class non-Koreans. Although neighbors shared in the struggle to make ends meet, the only Korean reinforcement Dan received was through his extended stepfamily. However, living in town allowed Dan's parents access to other Koreans. Although Dan did not interact directly with Koreans, his parents had only Korean friends, whom they entertained at their home. Thus, Dan had constant exposure to Korean Americans growing up, even if they did not live in his apartment complex.

In this part of the process, 1.5ers begin to experience two different conditions under which to express their ethnic options. At home they are able to express their Koreanness, and with their neighborhood and school friends they begin to express being Korean American and local. However, as I continue to discuss later in this chapter, the 1.5ers' experiences with their family and peers help them negotiate two ethnic divisions but also help to create a sense of shame for them. They begin to see their families as immigrants with whom they have to deal. One of the major obstacles that the 1.5ers face, and that other generations do not face, is language.

Transformation from Korean to Korean American

The Influence of Language

In the early part of the process, the 1.5ers do not know how to speak English. They know less English than their parents and are often dependent on them to make sense of the new language. However, the working-class parents, with their limited education, also have a difficult time speaking English. As the children begin to adapt to a new culture in Hawaiʻi, about a year after they immigrate, they become able to understand and communicate with others. Still, early on in the process English is still noticeably their second language and Korean their first language. The difference between the 1.5ers and their parents is that while the parents continue to speak Korean at home, the 1.5ers, especially those with siblings, are able to practice their English while still speaking Korean to their parents. Hence, early on they are still tied to their Koreanness yet begin to transform their sense of identity through their choice of language. Growing up with a working-class immigrant family, 1.5ers speak primarily Korean to their parents. As 1.5ers begin to experience speaking English, they bring their newfound language skills into their family.

Although the parents can understand some English, they have difficulty conversing fluently with non-Koreans. As a result, the parents continue to speak Korean at home to spouse, friends, relatives, and children. Furthermore, the type of jobs the working-class parents hold does not require them to be conversationally fluent. Jenny's father is a fisherman on a Korean fishing boat. He does have Samoan laborers on board, but he says that he just points and the men pull the net. Mr. Lee states that he can understand approximately 25 percent of English conversations; however, Mrs. Lee understands less. Andy's and Dan's fathers work for a taxi company. Their occupations do not require them to speak much to the customers. As long as they know the streets and locations where their customers want to go, they have little need to maintain conversations in English.

Their mothers also hold positions that require little or no English. Jenny's mom works at a hotel as a housekeeper, a job that does not require her to speak to the guests. In addition, the hotel has other Korean American women working, so her conversations with co-workers are in Korean. Andy's mom used to work in a manufacturing company where other Korean American women worked. But she found little time for conversations with her coworkers because she spent most of her day working on the assembly line. Dan's stepmother worked in a Korean restaurant as kitchen help. She associated only with Korean American women and never saw a need to speak English. Consequently, the parents who were able to understand some English found little requirement of the language in their daily lives.

Thus, the 1.5ers live in households where the parents speak Korean to their children, and the children speak Konglish and English to each other. The 1.5ers and their siblings speak English on matters that they do not want their parents to know about. Yet the 1.5ers admit that if it were not for their parents, they would not be bilingual today. The level of Korean proficiency among the siblings varies, with the eldest being the most fluent and the youngest understanding the language more than speaking it. However, it is not their age that makes them more fluent, but rather the need to speak Korean with their parents. The eldest child is given most of the household duties, and they pass on the responsibilities to the younger sibling if they are close in age. Jenny says that her older sister Jane quickly passed the bulk of the responsibilities to her. Andy, being the eldest, tried to pass the duties to his younger brother, but his brother "was not responsible." Therefore, Andy continues to care for both his siblings and his parents. Dan, an only child, continues to have the responsibility of translating information for his father. His father acknowledges how lonely being an only child was for Dan and states, "I want him to have five children so they don't grow up lonely." Dan thinks that it would have been easier for him if he had had siblings.

The 1.5ers state that they continue to speak Korean with their parents with a little bit of English. They say that speaking Korean with their parents is easier because there are certain feelings and expressions that cannot be expressed in English. In addition, the parents have incorporated certain English words into their vocabulary. In this part of the process the 1.5ers and their parents begin to transform their Koreanness to being more Korean American. The use of English and Konglish, and the shared understanding of who speaks what language to whom, is an indication of the change that Korean American families go through. Korean American 1.5ers begin actively to negotiate their ethnic boundaries by speaking Konglish and switching between Korean and English within the same family. In addition, the 1.5ers' observation of their parents' hard work and devotion to their education contributes to their continuation of Confucian practices emphasizing education, hard work, and respect for elders. The families thus participate in their 1.5ers' construction of a Korean American ethnic identity. Consequently, 1.5ers express their ethnic identity by pursuing higher or professional education, working long hours and sometimes two jobs to help their parents, and continuing to value their obligation to the family before themselves.

Changes in the Parent–Child Relationship

After young children immigrate to Hawai'i, they begin the process of becoming 1.5ers. Their memories of Korea and their inability to understand English help to sustain their Korean ethnicity. However, as they begin to interact with others outside the home, they start the process of transforming their identity from Korean to Korean American. While the 1.5ers experience changes in their lives, so do other family members. What changes the most for the working-class family is the relationship between the parents and children.

One of the changes that first-generation parents point out in their 1.5 generation children is their lack of investment in the family, the fact that the children put their friends and social life before their own family. However, this is not to say that 1.5ers do not care about their family; in fact, 1.5ers from working-class families appear to invest more of their time and energy into their homes than toward other children.

From an outsider's point of view, the 1.5ers may appear to be running the family functions. Because both parents typically work, the eldest 1.5ers initially have the role of taking care of their younger siblings when their parents are not at home. These 1.5ers are faced with responsibility early on in their life, having to cook and clean the home and supervise younger siblings. Jenny says that after her older sister relinquished her responsibility onto her, she was in charge of making sure her brother did his homework, asking him about his friends, and scolding him when the situation warranted. Andy has similar memories of growing up. He states that as the eldest he felt responsible for making sure that his siblings behaved while his parents were at work. Even when they returned home from work, he says that his mom was busy cooking and his dad was too tired to really talk to the kids. Andy felt that it was his responsibility to make sure that his siblings behaved for the sake of his parents. The 1.5ers like Jenny and Andy, who have younger siblings, are expected to help the family by taking charge. However, the added responsibility also adds stress to these "young" adults. Furthermore, the newfound relationships of the 1.5ers take away from the relationship that parents normally have with their children. The primary caregivers become the 1.5ers, which takes away from 1.5ers' ability to appreciate their childhood at home; thus, they often complain, "I never had a childhood."

In addition to taking care of their siblings, 1.5ers from working-class families take care of daily household functions. They act as interpreters, schedulers, and information gatherers in affairs that do not require the Korean language. Hence, the 1.5ers are needed more often than children of other generations and social classes. The parents depend on them for basic interactions with doctors, bill collectors, bankers, and other non–Korean-speaking representatives. Thus, the 1.5ers are left to cope with the realization that their parents are dependent on them, which makes it difficult for them to leave home, let alone the islands. They must deal with the fact that their parents cannot handle the daily living functions alone; they need someone who can serve as translator. Jenny currently lives with her parents and brother. She would like to move out, but she feels caught between her obligation to help her parents and her need to explore life. She states, "My parents can't speak English very well; in fact, they just don't speak it at all. I take care of their doctor's appointments, interpretation at various appointments, and handle the house bills. They are totally dependent on us [children] to take care of them." Although her forced responsibility often makes Jenny feel frustrated about her inability to lead her own life, her feelings of obligation demonstrate how Jenny has adopted notions of filial piety from her family. Her ethnic identity is tied to the Confucian ideology of considering the family over the self.

Andy states that he too worries about his family. While growing up he had to help out with the simple tasks of reading mail, screening calls for his parents, and helping his parents with basic English translations. Although Andy played an active role in helping his family function, he does not worry about whether his parents could make it in Hawai'i without him. For Andy, that is not an option. He says that growing up, he saw his parent sacrifice everything for him and his siblings. They never took a vacation or went out to eat at a nice restaurant, but just worked all the time so that the children could receive the "best" education and have the same opportunities as other children. His father "took insults daily" and although he did not speak English, managed to ask questions. Andy saw his mom wake up at 5:00 in the morning to prepare breakfast and lunch for the children and then go to work, only to return at 6:00 in the evening to prepare dinner and clean the house. Andy says that his parents worked nonstop and his contribution to the family was a necessity. He says, "My first goal is to help them retire" and when [my] father turns 60 in 1998, "I want to do the traditional banquet party thing." As a result of observing his parents' long hours at work, Andy has embraced the notion of filial piety and interprets his helping in the family as a way to show respect to his parents.

Dan states that he tries not to worry about his father, but fears that he will be all alone. With his father's recent separation from his third wife, Dan worries that there will be no one to take care of his father in his old age. A few years ago, Dan lived on his own until his father divorced from his second wife. Dan said that although his father was able to support himself, it was difficult for him, so he moved in to help out with the rent, basic costs of living, and daily household duties. He says, "It's just me and him, and we have to look out for each other." Dan says that growing up, he would help with interpreting English for his dad, but the bulk of his help to his father was financial. Dan says that he started working in his teens and went to machinist school, thinking that he would be able to make a lot of money. However, he found that he did not enjoy that line of work and went into tourism. But with Hawai'i's stagnant economy, Dan says that it is difficult to advance in the tourist industry. As a result, in late 1997 he began a business venture in hopes of "becoming a [millionaire] in a few years." He says that as soon as he makes it, he's going to buy his dad a home and take care of him so he can retire. Dan, like the other 1.5ers in this study, has adopted a sense of filial obligation.

The Korean American 1.5ers learn new roles in their working-class families. While the transformation from Korean to Korean American ethnicity takes place, 1.5ers also learn how to incorporate parts of Korean culture such as language and filial piety into their newly constructed Korean American ethnic identity.

The family serves as the place where the 1.5ers express their Koreanness more than anywhere else. Because of their parents and their parents' friends, the home is the place where 1.5ers are able to switch to the Korean mode of speech, behavior, and expressions. In addition, due to economic necessity, both parents typically work and require their children to help with managing the family. Korean American 1.5ers serve as mediators between their parents and the larger society, as translators, facilitators, and overall advocates for their parents. Furthermore, the 1.5ers help keep the family together by taking on the parents' role with their younger siblings. As a result of these added responsibilities, Korean American 1.5ers are able to maintain their Korean language abilities, appreciate the value of family, and maintain a sense of filial obligation.

Korean American 1.5ers' observation of their parents, relatives, and parents' friends, and their own experiences in their family contribute to their memories of being Korean and their ethnic transformation to Korean American. The family is a part of the process that affects how Korean American 1.5ers construct their 1.5 ethnic identity.

Case Studies of 1.5ers from Middle-Class Families

The subjects of the next three case studies, Hilary Kim, Travis Chung, and Pat Oh, help illustrate how middle-class families influence 1.5ers' construction of Korean and Korean American ethnic identities as part of the process of becoming 1.5ers.

HILARY KIM

Hilary Kim, 27 years old, immigrated to Hawai'i in 1974, when she was 2, with her mother. Hilary admits that although she immigrated when she was an infant, she does not identify as second generation and "obviously do[es not] identify with first generations." She expresses that she feels like she is in the middle of the two, a "1.5." Hilary's case reaffirms that 1.5ers are not restricted by their age of immigration and influenced me to reconfigure the term "1.5."

Although previous literature points to age at immigration as one of the criteria for 1.5ers, Hilary demonstrates that identity formation is not a rigid equation that can be measured methodologically. Hilary is conversationally bilingual, bicultural, and can situationally switch her identity from Korean to Korean American. In fact, Hilary can speak Korean better than many who came at age 9. She credits her parents and extended family for sustaining her Korean ethnicity. She has been raised predominantly as Korean in the home, eating Korean food, speaking Korean, showing respect to elders, entertaining Korean friends, interacting with relatives, partaking in Korean organizations, and being involved in the Korean community in Hawai'i. Hilary's case points to how critical the family is in maintaining a sense of Korean ethnic identity for 1.5ers.

Hilary says that her father came from a "good family" in Korea. He received his bachelor's and master's degrees from a prestigious university in Korea but never fulfilled his goal of pursuing graduate work in the United States. Hilary's mother graduated from high school but never pursued a college degree. In 1973, her father was on his way to Los Angeles on a student visa but stopped in Hawai'i to visit a friend. He ended up staying in Hawai'i and purchased a store and began a business venture. Hilary adds, "I think he borrowed money from his friend to get his business started." A year later, Hilary and her mother joined her father. Two years later, Hilary's sister, Susan, was born in Hawai'i and her paternal grandmother joined them there. Her father was the first to immigrate to the United States and later sponsored his siblings. Today, they have relatives spread throughout the United States.

Hilary attended private school all her life. Growing up, she tested for various private schools until she was accepted into Punahou. Her parents wanted her to attend the best school in Hawai'i and urged her to apply to Punahou when they heard of its prestige. After she graduated from high school, she attended a private university in Washington, D.C. Upon completing her bachelor's degree, she returned to Hawai'i and worked with her father for a year, and she is currently attending graduate school in Hawai'i. In 1999, she married her boyfriend, Steve (a 1.5er who also participated in this study). They moved to Washington, D.C., in 1999 and currently reside in Manhattan.

Travis Chung

Travis, 29 years old, immigrated to Hawai'i in 1976, when he was 7, with his brothers, Ben (32 years old),

Chris (27 years old), and Jon (23 years old), and his parents. His father graduated from high school, joined the merchant marines, and then worked as a laborer on a tanker truck in Korea. His mother graduated from high school and became a homemaker.

Their mother's younger brother, "small uncle," sponsored the Chung family. Travis' cousin was a boat captain who sailed from Korea to Fiji. On one of the trips, small uncle went to Fiji with him, met a Fijian, and was married. Small uncle and his new bride moved to Hawai'i and later sponsored the whole family. After they immigrated, Travis' father and mother both worked for the uncle, but later worked for a Korean-owned auto body shop.

Travis attended public school all his life, where he had largely 1.5 Asian American friends. After he graduated from high school, he attended the University of Hawai'i. He lived with his parents until he married his wife, Clariece, a hapa (Japanese and Caucasian) local girl. Clariece was attending college in the continental United States when a friend introduced them over the Internet. They maintained a long-distance relationship until she moved back to Hawai'i. Travis currently works as a financial manager, and Clariece works in a law firm. In the spring of 1998, they had a baby boy named Jarod.

Patrick Oh

Pat, 28 years old, immigrated to Hawai'i in 1977, when he was 7, with his older brother Jim (33 years old), sister Kathy (31 years old), and mother. Pat's father came from a wealthy family who owned a construction company. His father graduated from college and was a veterinarian. His mother graduated from high school and was a homemaker. However, after Pat's grandfather died, the family went bankrupt and lost everything. Because of financial stress, his parents divorced when Pat was 6. His mother decided to leave Korea due to the shame associated with divorce there.

Pat and his mother were sponsored by his step-aunt (the daughter of Pat's grandfather's second wife), who was married to a Caucasian in the military. During that time, Pat's aunt sponsored other family members; thus, he had various step-relatives in Hawai'i.

Growing up, Pat attended public schools where there were both Korean and local students. Pat, however, developed close relationships with the local Japanese. He then graduated from the University of Hawai'i and pursued a master's degree at a private university in Hawai'i. While attending graduate school, Pat lived with his mother and worked full-time in retail management to help his mother with her mortgage. Although Pat describes his relationship with his mother as "strong," he is not close to his extended-family members.

Pat feels that his sense of identity is intertwined with his sexuality. He is selectively openly gay, and often has to negotiate not only his ethnic identity but his sexuality as well. In 1998, Pat decided to move to San Francisco to explore his potential outside of Hawai'i. Today, Pat lives in San Francisco as a bank loan officer and has no immediate plans to return to Hawai'i.

Memories of Being an Immigrant

As discussed in Chapter 4, Korean American 1.5ers from middle-class families share feelings of marginalization and not fitting in. Memories of not understanding English are vivid for most, but what remains is the stigma of being an immigrant. As a result, Korean American 1.5ers start to disassociate from being Korean immigrants and sometimes try to pass as Hawaiian born or as another type of Asian American.

Whereas second-generation Korean Americans must cope with their ethnic social standing in Hawai'i, 1.5ers grow up having to deal with both their ethnic and immigrant status. They distance themselves from their immigrant and ethnic status by claiming that they are not like other Koreans. For Hilary, it was easier to pass as second-generation Korean American or even non-Korean. She says that she never really discussed her ethnicity at school because most of the students assumed that she was Chinese American. Travis, however, remembers being picked on by local students because he was an immigrant. He says that there was always conflict between the local Samoans, Hawaiians, and immigrant students. Pat recalls initially feeling "out of it," not understanding what others were saying but understanding their mocking action of "putting their fingers to their eyes, stretching them and saying 'ching chong.'" Like the working-class 1.5ers, these 1.5ers' early memories of how others perceived immigrants in general established clear boundaries between Locals and immigrants, with being an immigrant the less desirable ethnic option.

Neighborhood and Friends

In Hawai'i, there are visible markers of neighborhood segregation, mostly by class and ethnicity. The suburban areas, such as Kāhala, Wilhelmina Rise, and Hawai'i Kai, are composed of wealthy Caucasian, Japanese American, Chinese American, and Korean American families. In addition, there are certain exclusive, economically stratified high-rises in downtown Honolulu. There are scattered groups of otherwise socioeconomically disadvantaged minorities in these neighborhoods, but they are more the exception than the rule. Korean 1.5ers who grow up in these middle- to upper-class neighborhoods are exposed to predominantly educated Caucasians, Japanese Americans, and Chinese Americans in the neighborhood and in their schools. Caucasians, Chinese, and Japanese hold a higher position economically, occupationally, and educationally compared with other ethnic groups in Hawai'i. However, the perception in Hawai'i is that Japanese Americans are the most successful of all groups. Thus, for Korean Americans, the presence of Japanese Americans in prestigious positions, professions, and politics results in the belief that Japanese do indeed have as much power as Caucasians.

Hilary and her family lived in Honolulu most of their lives. After they immigrated to Hawai'i, they rented an apartment in town because it was close to her parents' store in Kalihi. After they were established, they purchased a condominium in an exclusive tower in Honolulu. The neighborhood they live in is multicultural, with some Korean Americans. However, it is not the neighborhood that exposes Hilary to Korean Americans, but her parents, their involvement in the Korean community, and her extended family. Although Hilary was only 2 when she immigrated to Hawai'i, she said that she grew up "doing the whole Korean thing, the dance and Korean American community stuff with my dad." Her father thought that in order to appreciate Korean culture, Hilary should learn to appreciate the arts. Hilary's parents focused on teaching her the language, values, and arts. Thus, they spoke Korean at home, enforced studying and respecting elders, and emphasized having a sense of decorum at all times. In addition, Hilary's father wanted her to be exposed to Korean American community affairs so that she was aware of the politics and the special events that occurred among Korean Americans. She says that in these functions, she interacted primarily with her parents' friends. The Korean American social circle consisted of first-generation Koreans much older than her. Hilary states that her parents were very much a part of the Korean American community in Hawai'i. Her father was an active member of Korean American community organizations and participated in various social and political activities. As a result, the Kim family attended Korean American functions regularly to support their father.

In addition, Hilary's aunt and uncle from her mother's side lived nearby, which allowed the Kim family to maintain their family rituals and traditions. At family gatherings, such as Korean Thanksgiving, Christmas, New Year's, and other Korean or American holidays, Hilary spoke primarily Korean, learned how to bow on New Year's, to cook and eat traditional Thanksgiving and New Year's food, and to maintain filial practices with her immediate and extended family members.

Travis lived in town most of his life. When his family immigrated, they stayed with their uncle, who is a successful businessperson in Honolulu. Although his mother continued to see her brother and even worked for him, Travis and his brothers rarely talked to him. They grew up renting homes in various parts of Honolulu, but as the children moved out and the economy declined, Travis' parents decided to move into state housing so that they could save money for their future. Travis, however, moved out of his parents' home before they moved into state housing. Travis lives in the outskirts of Honolulu in a high-rise condominium with his wife and newborn son.

Growing up, Travis had constant interaction with and exposure to his relatives. Travis and his brothers spoke Korean to first-generation relatives and their parents but spoke English to each other. Because of his extended family, Travis had constant reinforcement of Korean values, traditions, and culture. They had to show respect to their elders and participate in Korean holidays and rituals. In addition, his parents had mostly Korean friends and co-workers. Thus, Travis' identification was largely as Korean during the early part of the process.

When Pat and his family moved to Hawai'i, they lived with their step-aunt until his mom found work in retail sales. They then rented apartments in Honolulu until his brother and he got older. When Pat began working, he and his mother combined their savings and purchased a condominium in Mōili'ili. He says that it was difficult for his mother to pay the mortgage on her own, so he lived with her. Although they had an extended family in

Honolulu, Pat says that his exposure to them was limited. They would see each other on certain family gatherings, but overall their visits together were rare. Pat, however, feels that his mother has continued to practice Korean traditions in the home. He says, "She cooks Korean food almost every day and watches Korean television." Pat says that because his brother and mother speak Korean to each other and have mostly Korean friends, he was exposed to Korean people all his life. Pat was expected to show respect for his brother and other elders. In addition, Pat adopted the obligation to the good of the family and therefore gave a large portion of his income to them.

For the middle-class 1.5ers, the neighborhoods they lived in were multicultural with few immigrants. Although Travis' parents live in state housing, his experience growing up was with multicultural middle-class neighbors. However, it is not merely the neighborhood that influences 1.5ers' sense of ethnic identity but also other Korean Americans. The constant exposure to their parents' friends and extended families reaffirms the Korean influence. The 1.5ers' interaction with other first-generation Korean Americans reinforces their sense of being Korean. They are expected to bow before elders, offer them hospitality in their home, and show the overall respect that is expected from young Korean Americans. Such expectations are learned through observation but are also reinforced by their parents. For example, their parents will ask them to serve guests refreshments and show hospitality at all times.

Transformation from Korean to Korean American

THE INFLUENCE OF LANGUAGE

One of the main barriers for immigrant families is language. Because the majority of family members and their parents' friends spoke little to no English, Korean American

1.5ers were indirectly forced to continue using the Korean language. However, for middle-class families the barrier is reduced because at least one of the parents is able to speak English fairly fluently. Consequently, Korean American 1.5ers from middle-class families at this part of the process tend to speak Korean to the less fluent parent but speak Konglish to their more fluent parent and siblings. Thus, 1.5ers learn early on how to express and negotiate between Korean and Korean American ethnic identities.

As Korean American 1.5ers grow up, middle-class families encourage their children to watch both Korean and American television, but stress *Sesame Street* over Korean children's shows. The parents' interest in their children's education is similar to that of the working-class parents; however, middle-class parents also stress that their children attend the best schools or most prestigious institutions. The parents do not want their children to be disadvantaged by not having the same opportunities as other middle-class children.

Due to the constant exposure to extended family and family friends, 1.5ers use Korean in the home. They speak Korean and Konglish with various family members and learn through the social interactions the expected behaviors and values. Korean American 1.5ers learn from their family, relatives, and family friends how to interact with other Korean Americans. The use of honorific language and bowing to guests and elders reveal 1.5ers' understanding of Korean social cues and behaviors. In addition, they learn that their behaviors are a reflection on not only them but on their parents also. Thus, 1.5ers act accordingly so that they do not shame their parents. Hilary states that growing up, she spoke primarily Korean at home until she entered preschool. The concentration on Korean language at home was influenced by her grandmother's role in raising Hilary and her younger sister. In order to communicate with their grandmother, they had to speak Korean. Furthermore, her parents spoke primarily Korean to her. It was not until she entered school that she began to learn English and then started using it with her family. However, Hilary states that it is just easier to communicate certain thoughts and feelings in Korean. In addition to speaking Korean, she is attuned to Korean behavioral cues and cultural nuances. For example, she knows not to disagree openly with her parents in front of their friends; she knows that when pouring tea or drinks, she has to pour for the eldest first; and she acknowledges showing respect for her parents at all times in public. She claims to have learned all of these values growing up in a Korean family with "very Korean parents and grandmother." Although she speaks Korean to all of her relatives and her mother, she states that she speaks Konglish with her father. She says that her choice is based on what language the person is speaking. She says that because her father is fairly fluent in English, she can speak Konglish with him. When words that she does not know in Korean come up in their conversation, she will use English. When there is a Korean expression that can express what she is feeling, she speaks Korean. She says, "There are some things that sound better in Korean than English." She and her father have more serious conversations about her school, politics, and community affairs in English. With her mother, however, she speaks primarily Korean. Though her mother has lived in Hawai'i for over 20 years, she is still not fluent or comfortable speaking English. Hilary thinks it has to do with the fact that her mother socializes only with Koreans, which impedes her English abilities. As a result, her conversations with her mother are limited to informal talks, and they rarely discuss political or community issues unless her father is present. Thus, she continues to speak Korean to her mother and grandmother, and Konglish to her father. She says, "There are certain words that are just not the same in English, and it's just easier to talk to them in a language that they are comfortable with." Hilary, like other 1.5ers, adapted to her parents' utilization of the language that is most comfortable for them.

She learned, at this part of the process of becoming a 1.5er, that she is able to switch not only her language in various settings but her ethnic options as well. She says, "Sometimes it feels like I have multiple lives. At home, with my parents, I am the obedient Korean daughter. I do the obligatory Korean thing and obey my parents' rules. But outside, with my friends, I'm totally different. I mean, I act totally different . . . (laughs) I'm just totally different (laughs)."

Hilary says that although her filial obligations are carried out in the home, outside with her non-Korean friends she is more relaxed and easygoing, and not conscious of behaving properly. Her ability to negotiate her "two lives" demonstrates her ability to switch between Korean and Korean American ethnic identities. She is able to express the values of respect and decorum to her parents and relatives while articulating a Korean American identity with her non-Korean friends. Thus, what becomes a part of her identity are facets and expressions of Korean and Korean American ethnic identities.

Travis recalls struggling with the English language and having to take special classes outside of school so that he could learn how to speak English. He says, "When I was growing up in Makiki, when I was younger, there was more prejudice. . . . They had more scuffles with the Vietnamese and with Koreans, they just called us 'yobos.'" Travis' Korean accent often made him the target of ridicule from local children, and as a result, he was insecure about himself. He went to Kaimanu English as a Second Language class, and his mother arranged a private tutor for 2 years so that he could continue practicing his English. At this early part of the process, Travis felt alienated as a Korean in Hawai'i. However, as he became fluent in English, he gained confidence and began to express more of a Korean American ethnic identity.

At home, Travis began to speak English with his brothers, and Korean and Konglish with his parents. He says that both of his parents are fairly fluent in English, but his mother speaks more English at work. His father's job as a taxi driver does not require much conversation in English. His mom, however, works in retail sales and is in a position to speak Korean, English, and some Japanese. Consequently, his mother's daily interaction with customers has made her more fluent in English than his dad.

Pat also remembers struggling with English. His memories of being teased for the way he spoke and looked remain with him. He says that he looked like a "chuntugi," a country bumpkin. He says that if he had known what the kids were saying earlier, he may have learned to dress differently. It was not until he began to understand English that he was picked on not for his English ability but just for his overall appearance. He states that speaking English was a method by which he demonstrated to his peers that he was indeed "Americanized."

At home, the Oh family spoke primarily Korean. Pat says that his brother was 5 years older when they immigrated and therefore never lost his Korean accent. As a result, his brother identified with first-generation Korean Americans more than the 1.5ers. Thus, at home Pat's mom and brother spoke Korean while Pat spoke Konglish to both of them. He said that when relatives came over to their house, he would speak primarily Korean, but felt comfortable expressing himself in Konglish to his family. He said that it had a lot to do with the fact that his mom and brother both were fairly fluent. Although they had a Korean accent, they were able to carry on conversations in English. Thus, Pat was able to take advantage of both English and Korean when he wanted to express a certain feeling or thought. The use of Korean and English in the home became a way for Pat and other 1.5ers to express their Korean American 1.5 ethnic identity.

Korean American middle-class families speak Konglish and Korean in the home. Unlike the working-class families, at least one parent from the middle-class family is fairly fluent in English, which allows the children to speak Konglish not only to their siblings but to one of the parents as well. However, 1.5ers continue to speak Korean with a parent or with relatives who feel more comfortable speaking Korean. Hence, 1.5ers adapt and speak the language that is most comfortable to others. In addition, by speaking Korean to first-generation Koreans, the 1.5ers are in fact carrying on a part of the culture. While 1.5ers can speak with respect in English, the Korean language has a separate honorific style of speech, which 1.5ers use to address those who are older. Thus, by speaking Korean, 1.5ers are able to demonstrate their cultural understanding of the importance of respect to elders, a value that becomes an integral part of their ethnic identity.

CHANGES IN THE PARENT–CHILD RELATIONSHIP

Middle-class parents do not stress speaking only Korean, nor do they need to. Whereas working-class parents depend on their bilingual children to help with household tasks, middle-class parents do not rely on their 1.5 children in the same way. Because one parent speaks English fairly fluently, the 1.5ers have more time to pursue other activities. However, they continue to help out with general household duties.

While growing up, middle-class 1.5ers receive guidance and structure from their parents. The rules and household functions are dictated and managed by the parents. Although the 1.5ers help, the parents are not as dependent on them to run the household. Thus, 1.5ers from middle-class families are left to think more about their own personal goals and worry less about whether their parents could function without them.

Hilary states that her relationship with her parents has been "normal" in that she asked them for permission to do things, for money, and for advice on schools and jobs. Her parents kept her and her sister active in the Korean American community, so in many ways her parents dictated the types of activities in which she was involved. Consequently, Hilary was also involved in the Korean community, took Korean dancing classes, and participated in various cultural activities. Her choices in Korean activities had to do with her parents' recommendations, and at the same time, growing up in an active family, Hilary saw that as a part of the norm.

Travis adds that although both of his parents worked, they also managed the house. Growing up, he never had to help with paying the bills, reading the mail, or translating for his parents. He states that his parents were self-sufficient. However, because both of his parents worked, Travis had to care for his two younger brothers. His older brother relinquished his duties to Travis when he was 8 years old, and since then he has felt responsible for his two younger brothers. As a result, he was expected to discipline his brothers for their behaviors and performance at school. Thus, his responsibility was largely related to raising his brothers.

Pat says that he did not have the average relationship with his mother, largely because she had to be both mother and father to him. After they immigrated to the states, Pat's father died of cancer. When he was growing up, his only father figure was his older brother, who served as the disciplinarian. Pat says that his relationship with his mother has always been good but distant. It was difficult to have a close relationship with her because she worked most of the time. As a result, the children usually fended for themselves. His mother would have Korean food prepared and ready for them in the refrigerator. Pat says that because he was not the youngest, the household duties were left mostly to his brother. However, as he got older and after his brother married, his mother began to rely more on Pat to help out at home.

Pat says that because he worked most of his life, his relationship with his mother was fairly egalitarian. Though he respected her for "never going on welfare and working her butt off," he did not have a mother who was waiting for him after school either. Pat always felt that all the members of the family were self-sufficient but helped each other out. Pat's decision to leave Hawai'i was not difficult because he knew that his mother "is a survivor" and capable of taking care of herself. He said that if his mother was not educated or literate, he might not have left for San Francisco to pursue his own goals.

The middle-class parents' hard work and dedication to their children's future lead 1.5ers to do well in school and pursue better professional opportunities. All of the case study subjects recognized how their parents sacrificed their own goals and dreams in order to provide for the family. Hilary saw how her father sacrificed his own dreams of attending graduate school for the sake of his children, and she admires him for it. While Hilary attends graduate school in Hawai'i, she states that her parents have taught her to make goals and pursue them. With Hawai'i's stagnant economy, Hilary is planning to move to Washington, D.C. With her upcoming marriage and possible family, opportunities are more available in the continental states than in Hawai'i.

Travis states that he has much respect for his parents. Although his parents came from a middle-class background and lived a fairly comfortable life in Korea, they left so that their four sons could pursue a better life. Travis points out how his father works as a taxi driver and his mother works in retail, positions that they acquired to help support the children. Travis states that he admires his parents for working so hard and instilling in him the desire to make goals and pursue them. He said that before getting married, he planned to attend graduate school, and he still hopes to pursue that goal in the future. However, with a new child he states that he is looking into pursuing a better job in the state of Washington or California. He says that the cost of living and job opportunities are better outside of Hawai'i, and therefore he is planning to move soon.

Middle-class Korean American 1.5ers struggle with their ethnic identity. Their experiences remind them of the discrimination they faced growing up as immigrants. However, as they became fluent in English they were more exposed to non-immigrant youth in their schools and neighborhoods. Thus, 1.5ers transform their ethnic identity from Korean to Korean American.

The emphasis on their Korean ethnic identity is reinforced through their interactions with and observations of other first-generation Koreans, their extended family members, and family friends. Through these interactions, the 1.5ers learn the social etiquette of interacting with those who are older, with men and women, and treating everyone as a guest. In addition, 1.5ers appreciate their parents' sacrifices for their future. Their parents' emphasis on education, social mobility, and success teach 1.5ers to pursue their educational and professional goals. They maintain their respect for their parents and at the same time strive for their individual goals. Thus, the combination of filial practices and individual goals reflect the construction of a Korean American ethnic identity.

Korean American 1.5ers from middle-class families are not as crucial to the family functioning as those from the working-class families are. While these 1.5ers may help one parent with translations or helping out with their younger siblings, the household duties of paying bills, reading mail, and so on are done by the parents. Thus, the middle-class parents are less dependent on their children to help with managing the family than working-class parents are. This has much to do with the fact that in the middle-class families, at least one of the parents is fairly fluent in English. Therefore, the 1.5ers speak not only Korean to their parents but Konglish as well. Because of the parent's ability to speak English somewhat fluently, 1.5ers are able to have intricate discussions about their plans and goals.

Furthermore, because the middle-class parents are more self-sufficient and less dependent on their children, the 1.5ers do not worry about whether the parents will be able to manage on their own. Whereas working-class children worry over the future of their parents and plan to take care of them themselves, the middle-class 1.5ers do not voice the same type of concerns. The 1.5ers from middle-class families do not worry about their parents' retirement because they know that they have secure plans for their future. Hence, knowing that their parents are financially taken care of and are able to manage without the translation or household assistance of their children makes it easier for the 1.5ers to pursue their own goals. Pat has already moved to San Francisco to pursue his goals, and Hilary and Travis have both expressed their plans to move in the next year. Because they do not have to worry about their parents' welfare, it is easier for them to strive for their own goals. Thus, middle-class 1.5ers are more independent largely because their parents are less dependent on them. However, their independence does not mean that they are less filial. Middle-class 1.5ers demonstrate their filial obligations differently than the working-class 1.5ers. For middle-class parents, their 1.5 children's success is a direct reflection on the family and brings pride to the family.

The 1.5ers learn from their families the value of education, hard work, and family. While the family stresses Korean culture to their children by keeping it in the home, the 1.5ers' experiences of growing up in a first-generation Korean family learn what it means to be a Korean American. The use of Konglish and pursuing one's own endeavors are both Korean and Korean American traits that become a part of their 1.5 ethnic identity.

6

STEREOTYPES AND THEIR
IMPACT ON ETHNIC
IDENTITY FORMATION

The history of Korean immigration to the United States spans approximately a century. Officially since 1902, Korean immigrants have established communities and situated themselves in Hawai'i. Although the greatest influx of Korean immigration occurred after 1965, with the majority of Koreans settling in New York, Chicago, and Los Angeles, Hawai'i has the longest and richest history of Korean American communities. Although there are two distinct "types" of Korean Americans in Hawai'i—those who have been here since the plantation era and those who arrived since the 1965 Immigration Act—the more visible construction of a Korean American community did not occur in Hawai'i until the late 1970s and early 1980s, when the post-1965 immigrants positioned themselves there.

Although family influences the 1.5er's identification with being Korean and Korean American, the presentation of the Korean American community in Hawai'i and the impressions held by the larger Hawai'i society also affect how 1.5ers identify with being Korean American and/or local. Stereotypes of Korean Americans in Hawai'i are prevalent among schools, peers, local media, and non–Korean Americans, contributing to 1.5ers' disassociation from other Korean Americans in Hawai'i.

The stereotypes of Korean Americans are largely influenced by the perception of Keʻeaumoku Street and Waikīkī as representative of the Korean American community. The larger society holds images of Korean Americans as aggressive, rude, hot-tempered, and holding jobs as bar hostesses and taxi drivers. Such stereotypes have branded Korean Americans and have had negative consequences for 1.5ers. Under such conditions, 1.5ers distance themselves from Koreans and associate with non-Koreans. The shame and embarrassment they feel as a result of the stereotypes discourages them from identifying with Koreans.

Korean American 1.5ers also learn what it means to be Korean American or local from their non–Korean peers at junior high and high school. With the dominant stereotypes of Korean Americans hovering over them, they learn of alternative ethnic options to identify with in order to disassociate themselves from the label held by the larger society. This chapter examines how the Korean American community is perceived by the local society and how such stereotypic perceptions affect 1.5ers' identification with being Korean American. Furthermore, this chapter will examine the role of non–Korean American peers in constructing alternative ethnic options as Korean American and local.

Perceptions of the Korean American Community: "Koreamoku" Is Us?

The Korean American business community in Hawaiʻi currently concentrates on and markets to the first generation and Korean tourists. Hence, signs and advertisements are in Korean, and most of the businesses employ Korean Americans.

Ask any Korean American or local person in Hawaiʻi where one can find Korean businesses, restaurants, or more generally the Korean American community, and most, if not all, will point to Keʻeaumoku Street (Keʻeaumoku) and Waikīkī. Keʻeaumoku is in the heart of Honolulu, near the Ala Moana Shopping Center and Waikīkī, and stretches into a residential section of Makiki. The commercial area is a busy area of town where there is a combination of local and tourist foot and car traffic. In the last 5 years, Keʻeaumoku has become more Korean, so much that non-Koreans refer to it as "Koreamoku." There are restaurants, acupuncturists, golf stores, insurance offices, and liquor stores that bear Korean signs and are run by Koreans. There is a strong presence in Keʻeaumoku, unlike other areas in Honolulu, of Korean American representation. Keʻeaumoku, even to the non-local eye, is clearly filled with Korean merchants and businesses. Korean restaurants, in particular the "yakiniku" barbecue restaurants, once were the primary signs of Korean business, but today there are competing restaurants, coffee shops, bakeries, dry cleaners, tailors, sports card dealers, games and gun dealers, and retail stores, as well as other types of businesses.

As one walk or drives along Keʻeaumoku, one sees a number of restaurants, shops, and other businesses with Korean language signs. However, the more visible Korean signs appear in pockets, in small plazas along Keʻeaumoku that house mostly Korean businesses. For example, Sam Sung Plaza has become more Korean since 1997. In the mid-1990s, Sam Sung Plaza included the Sam Sung store, a Japanese restaurant, a Japanese bookstore, a karaoke bar, a cosmetics store, and a Korean restaurant with no visible sign. There was nothing distinctive about this plaza, except for the Sam Sung store's reputation for carrying reasonably priced electronics. As the Korean economy developed and tourists started visiting the islands, the plaza began to reshape itself. The electronics store was renovated into a department store, and a Korean bakery and juice bar, alterations store, herbal store, and dry cleaner emerged with Korean signs. What was once a nondescript plaza in three years became more distinctively

Korean. With the recent economic decline of Korea, the plaza has added Japanese signs to its businesses. Each intersection after Sam Sung Plaza houses pockets of Korean merchants and businesses with predominantly Korean signs and Korean workers. Keʻeaumoku has become a smaller version of Koreatown in Los Angeles, what some Locals are starting to refer as "Koreamoku," although Korean Americans have not adopted this term. The notion of Keʻeaumoku representing the Korean American community has generated mixed reactions among Korean Americans.

Is Keʻeaumoku or Waikīkī Representative of the Korean American Community and Its People?

From the early 1970s to the present, Keʻeaumoku has been known for its restaurants and drinking establishments, known by Locals as "Korean bars." These bars employ Korean American and other hostesses, who make their rounds, hook up with male customers, and ask them to buy them a drink. The hostesses are tipped by the patron to sit with the customers and drink and in some cases receive a percentage of drink sales. The "Korean bars" have become such an integral part of the local community that people often equate hostess bars with Koreans, and thus the name "Korean bar" has emerged. In the newspapers, television, and local discussions, references to "Korean bars" have occurred much more frequently than the Korean American community would like. There are several implications to this term. First, it portrays Korean Americans, especially women, as sexually loose, "bar girl" types who want their patrons to buy them a "drinkie drinkie." Second, it gives the impression that Koreans are primarily involved in a type of business that is marginally close to prostitution.

As a result, a group of first-generation Korean Americans pressured the press and television media to stop using the term *Korean bar* in their news stories. A University of Hawai'i historian states that social pressure from first-generation Koreans has resulted in a change from the term *Korean bar* to *hostess bar*. Although the media does not commonly use the term Korean bar any more, it is still used regularly by Locals. Regardless of whether a bar is Korean owned, the idea of a "Korean bar" is now a part of the larger society's vocabulary.

In the May 19, 1998, *Honolulu Star-Bulletin*, Bill Kwon, a sports reporter, wrote of the recent victory of a Korean American golfer. This article sparked much anger from the Korean Jaycees. The article reads, "They're dancing in the streets of Seoul. And, I imagine, on Ke'eaumoku St. too; especially during happy hour; and Who knows? Maybe there even might be a Club Se Ri on Ke'eaumoku St. some day." In response to this article, John, a Jaycees member, wrote an e-mail to the editor stating,

> *We are not exactly sure what Mr. Kwon was trying to express in these sentences, but one can't help but think that all Koreans live on Ke'eaumoku, or that all Koreans attend "happy hours," or that all Koreans engage in liquor businesses (i.e., "Club Se Ri"). What is most certain, however, is that Mr. Kwon's comments stereotype Korean Americans as being at least associated with these activities. In effect and in a subtle way, Korean Americans are attributed with socially undesirable characteristics. We sincerely question Mr. Kwon's judgment in making these statements. It is possible that Mr. Kwon was trying to add humor to his article; however, this type of humor is not only offensive to Korean Americans but can lead to racist treatment toward Korean Americans.*

Another Jaycees member, Don, wrote through e-mail, "As you can imagine, this is not very culturally sensitive, and is offensive to many Koreans who are disturbed by the association that people make with Koreans and the 'hostess bars' in Hawai'i." Immediately, the editor replied, "I agree with you. The remarks were offensive and never should have been published. The fact that Bill is of Korean ancestry does not make it acceptable. I apologize and will see to it that those responsible are aware of your displeasure and mine" (5/20/98 e-mail).

Stereotypical comments about Korean Americans such as these are common in Hawai'i. Hilary adds that although her immigrant status was a source of shame for her, what still embarrasses her to date is the stereotype of the Korean bar hostess. Hilary states,

> *In Hawai'i, the ongoing thing is that Koreans own hostess bars and that Korean women work in these establishments. The thing is, why do they have to focus on the hostess bars? I mean, there is so much more to the community than the hostess bars, but that is what we are linked to. They never talk about Korean doctors, lawyers, or other professionals. It's always the Korean hostess bars.*

Hilary states that there are also Thai, Vietnamese, Filipino, and Caucasian hostesses, yet whenever people talk about these bar workers, Koreans are the ones associated with them. She states that such a stereotype of Korean American women not only gives the wrong impression but perpetuates the image of them as sex workers and consequently has more negative implications for Korean American women than men. She says that if the stereotypes were more positive, like those of Japanese and Caucasians as being rich, it would not be as bad. The Korean bar hostess stereotype is only one example of how the ethnic identity of Korean American 1.5ers and the second generation is affected. Articles in the newspaper and the prevailing stereotypes are mere reminders of the label that is their source of embarrassment and shame.

Waikīkī, a major tourist destination, has also gone through some changes in the last decade. For tourists, Waikīkī represents Hawai'i: hotels, shops, restaurants, clubs, and other retail businesses catering to tourists. In the heart of Waikīkī, the International Market Place has been in business for decades. It consists of small vendors, spread throughout an outside mall, selling various goods such as jewelry, Hawaiian artifacts, aloha wear, candles, and other tourist souvenirs. Since the 1970s, this area has housed predominantly Korean American vendors who cater to tourists, often selling goods at prices far above their worth and haggling with clients to make them feel that they got a bargain. In the 1980s, the International Market Place faced the possibility of a proposed convention center replacing its space. Korean American merchants demonstrated in front of the market to discourage the construction. While merchants mobilized together, the method by which they demonstrated became a topic in the local community. These first-generation merchants had several factors that worked against them in their demonstration. First, there was the language barrier. Most of the merchants did not speak English or spoke with a heavy accent; therefore, when the news media came to interview them, they were not able to express their views to the larger community. Second, the demonstration tactics they used were those that were common in Korea. They used blood, or red paint that looked like blood, to make signs protesting the construction. However, to non–Korean eyes, the demonstrators were unsettling as they cut their fingers to write their signs, crying and screaming in Korean. This image presented an uncivilized picture of Korean merchants as irrational and barbaric. The symbolism behind this sign-making demonstration reveals how important the businesses and their locations are to the merchants. The blood symbolizes the blood and sweat that the merchants put into their work and how their businesses are connected to their livelihood. It is unclear if it was the demonstration that secured the fate of the International Market Place, but the convention center did not take its place.

The image of Korean American merchants in the International Market Place has influenced the way tourists and people in Hawai'i view Koreans. The impression is that Koreans in Hawai'i are mostly first-generation, small vendors who "wheel and deal" in an aggressive manner. Although it is true that Koreans do dominate the marketplace, vending is not the primary source of income for Korean Americans. The aggressive nature of vendors contributes to the stereotype of money-hungry Koreans. In addition, the protest tactics of Korean Americans have perpetuated the image of a foreign community in Hawai'i. Hence, for the Korean American 1.5 and second generations, such impressions represent another layer contributing to others' sense of their ethnic identity, and another image to distance themselves from and try to change.

The International Market Place is still in business; however, the ethnic composition of the vendors has changed. There has been an increase of Vietnamese merchants. There are still many Korean American merchants, but in the last 5 years merchants have been selling their spaces to secure larger ones in hotels, in shopping complexes, department stores, and along the main strip of Kalākaua Avenue in Waikīkī. It is a sign of moving up from a small cart in a marketplace to an enclosed retail space. Five years ago, the primary foreign language spoken or written on business doors in Waikīkī was Japanese. Today, the presence of Koreans and Korean writing on businesses has increased due to the large presence of Korean tourist shoppers. However, the influx of Korean tourists has dropped, and it is unclear how this will alter the presentation of shops in Waikīkī.

Implications of the Current Image of the Korean American Community

Although Ke'eaumoku Street and Waikīkī have the most visible signs of a Korean American community, they are not representative of the heterogeneous community. There are businesses, retail stores, and restaurants scattered throughout O'ahu. There are growing communities in Mililani, a suburban area 15 miles from Honolulu; on Makiki, an area that is about 2 miles from Ke'eaumoku Street; and in Kalihi, a working-class area of Honolulu, 5 miles from Ke'eaumoku. These areas, however, are often left out of the discussion of the Korean American community. Even more conspicuously absent from the local and Korean American community discourse is the presentation of non–Korean-focused businesses. The impression is that only those businesses that bear *hangul* (Korean) signs are Korean owned. Sean Chung states that there are doctors, chiropractors, lawyers, and other professionals who do not work under a Korean marquee, yet they are not included in how Korean Americans are viewed in Hawai'i.

Aside from the visible signs of a Korean American community, the people who lead the community are a primary source of how Koreans are presented in Hawai'i. Having Korean signs on businesses can have diverse effects. First, it attracts and calls out to first-generation Koreans to patronize these businesses. Second, it sends a message to the predominantly Korean-speaking first generation that at these businesses one does not have to speak English and can communicate effortlessly to purchase what one wants. Third, the signs reflect a message that there is a sense of pride in being Korean and owning a business. They are markers for the Korean American community that the establishments are owned by Korean merchants and businesspeople who have established themselves in Hawai'i.

On the other side, the presence of a Korean marquee may lead some to suspect Koreans' tendency to exclude non-Koreans. The local Japanese, Chinese, and Filipino communities do not market their ethnicity to the community to the same extent. Businesses that bear Korean language signs also have Korean-speaking employees who are perceived by Locals and 1.5 and second-generation

Korean Americans as more cordial to Koreans than to other ethnic groups. Pat echoes such impressions, stating, "Koreans have a bad habit of exclusively associating with other Koreans. They don't have a diverse group of friends. There's a distinction between those [1.5 and second generation] with a diverse group of friends and those without [first generation]."

Pat's reference to Koreans is directed at first-generation Korean Americans. Because the larger community interacts with and sees more of the first-generation business community, they may assume that all Koreans are exclusive. The 1.5ers state that the Korean signs and businesses that employ Korean-speaking employees send the signal that if one does not speak Korean, one should not patronize these businesses. Though this is not necessarily the intent of the signs, for any business wants customers regardless of ethnicity, the Korean business community up to now has marketed itself to the first generation without clear consideration of non-Koreans in the local community.

The misrepresentation of Korean Americans is further perpetuated by the limited exposure to other Korean businesses and professionals. For the Korean American 1.5 and second generations, it is difficult to express positive images of Korean Americans. Pat states, "It's easier to think about the bad things. We only see the negative image of the Korean culture." The predominant first-generation Korean American community image contributes to the division between generations and to the alienation felt by the 1.5 and second generations.

There are several organizations that have represented the Korean American community. They are the United Korean Society (UKS), KBFD-TV and KCBH-TV, the Korean Chamber of Commerce, and three newspapers: *Seoul Daily News Hawai'i, Korea Times,* and *Korea Central Daily of Hawai'i.* These organizations have members and subscribers who keep them in "business." Korean Americans and non-Koreans view the first-generation organizations and their members as the primary representatives of the Korean American community.

The United Korean Society allows anyone interested in the welfare of the community to become a registered member. The person does not have to be Korean but must show interest in the organization and the Korean American community. This organization has officers and is considered by the State of Hawai'i as an organization that can help and lead the Korean American community. In the 1997 *Korean Directory of Hawai'i*, which the UKS publishes, Governor Benjamin Cayetano praised the organization for its work in providing "valuable information and ready access to a wide range of services and community." He adds that the publication creates closer ties among Korean Americans in the islands by uniting them to a common purpose. The governor, like other residents of Hawai'i, assumes that the UKS is the leading voice and most active organization in helping the Korean American community. However, the UKS assists mostly first-generation Korean Americans by providing translation help, immigration assistance, and even transportation for nondriving older members. Although the Hawaiian community assumes that the UKS serves and represents all of the generations in the Korean American community, it is run by and caters to first-generation Korean Americans. The main problem is that there is a limited representation of community members in the organization. The different generations of Korean Americans are not represented in its membership; the majority of members are first generation and their children whom the parents have convinced to join. The significance of membership is that only registered members are allowed to vote in the elections for officers; thus those leading the organization do not reflect the true needs and desires of the general Korean American community but only those of the active membership.

Though the UKS has limited interaction with 1.5 and second-generation Korean Americans and non-Koreans in Hawai'i, the organization is perceived by the state and even by the Korean government as the primary link between Korea and Korean Americans in Hawai'i. Thus, the UKS is looked to by the larger society as the voice of Korean Americans in Hawai'i. Hence, though they welcome all who are interested in the organization, it deflects other Korean Americans such as the 1.5 generation and second-generation Koreans from participating.

The three local Korean newspapers are an integral part of the community. They publicize community events, and social and political happenings in Hawai'i and in Korea, and they run various ads for local Korean businesses. In many ways, the newspapers serve as the link between Korea and Hawai'i, keeping Korean Americans in Hawai'i abreast of the sociopolitical situations "back home." The focus of the newspapers is dominated by stories about Korea, which in some ways may perpetuate the views of Koreans in Hawai'i as nationalistic and patriotic. The newspapers are in *hangul*, and this for the nonliterate Koreans is not an option. Like the UKS, the newspapers cater to first-generation Koreans. The newspapers' lack of non–Korean/local involvement presents Korean Americans as non-American and suggests that the interests of Koreans in Hawai'i continue to be with Korea, which perpetuates the "us versus them" mentality. Finally, the papers exclude not only non-Koreans, but 1.5ers and others who are not as invested in Korean and first-generation issues.

If we were to look at the UKS and Korean newspapers as the voice of Koreans in Hawai'i, we would assume that first-generation Koreans are characteristic of all Korean Americans. The 1.5ers themselves have bought into the stereotypical images of Koreans in Hawai'i. When asked to describe Koreans in Hawai'i, 1.5ers state that Korean Americans are "materialistic," "hot-tempered," "forward," "narrow-minded," "ethnocentric," "outspoken," "too much into saving face," "too gossipy," "judgmental," "conservative," "backwards," and "chauvinistic."

138

Korean American 1.5ers do not paint a positive picture of Koreans in Hawai'i. When this is pointed out to them, they also note the various model minority stereotypes of Korean Americans as hard-working and dedicated to the family, but what flow more freely are the negative characteristics of Koreans. What is significant about these negative images of first-generation Korean Americans is that the 1.5ers do not see them as characterizing themselves. When 1.5ers describe the characteristics of Korean Americans, they are describing the first generation or Korean nationals. In the process of becoming 1.5, the stereotypical images influence the way 1.5ers think about being Korean American and consequently lead to shame and embarrassment over being Korean.

The face of the Korean American community has changed and will continue to transform with each generation. The image of the community, however, is still dominated by how local/mainstream society views Korean Americans. Unfortunately, the impressions of Koreans are based primarily on stereotypes and images provoked by Ke'eaumoku Street and Waikīkī. Such stereotypes are internalized not only by non-Koreans; 1.5ers in the process of becoming 1.5ers themselves adopt these stereotypes. As a result of internalizing the stereotypes, 1.5ers conclude that Korean Americans are a group to be ashamed of. Thus, their understanding of what it means to be Korean American is connected to the larger society's views of Korean Americans.

Education and Peers

While 1.5ers learn what it means to be Korean American from the larger society's stereotypes of the first generation, they also learn what it means to be Korean American/local from their interactions with peers at school. The types of schools 1.5ers attend and their ethnic compositions have much to do with the area in which the

1.5ers live. For working-class parents, their limited educational experience makes it difficult for them to see the qualitative difference between public and private schools. Still, working-class parents encourage their 1.5 children to attend school, graduate, and attend either a professional or vocational school or college. Jenny's father, Mr. Lee, states that he always regretted not getting his high school diploma and pursuing an education. Although he made enough to send his children to private school, he felt that the most important thing was that his children received a college education.

Public and Private Schools: Peers and Their Influence on Korean American/Local Ethnic Identity

Korean American 1.5ers who attend public schools have more exposure to other Korean Americans and pidgin-speaking Locals than those who attend private schools. However, their internalized stereotypes of Korean Americans as "fresh off the boat," or "FOB," deter the 1.5ers from fostering relationships with other Korean Americans. Despite the presence of other 1.5ers in public schools, at this time in the process one is not aware of the uniqueness of being a 1.5er, but is more concerned with society's impressions of Korean Americans. These stereotypes and views held by the local community influence the 1.5ers' choice to disassociate from their Korean ethnicity and seek an alternative Korean American or local identity. The 1.5ers who attend private schools have limited exposure to Korean Americans. Instead their interactions are with local Asian Americans who do not speak pidgin on a regular basis. Thus, these 1.5ers adopt more of the "American" identity, an identity that is not Korean Korean or local. They speak standard English, are focused on entering a prestigious university, and express themselves as more "American," which some refer to as being more "*haole*" than local.[1] Thus, there are clear differences in the types of students 1.5ers are exposed to and influenced by in their schools.

IMMIGRANTS OR "FOBS"

Generally, 1.5ers remember what it was like to be "FOB" at school. The memories of not understanding English, being picked on for their dress, and being the new immigrant student are still vivid for 1.5ers. Their experiences at school are just one part of the process of becoming 1.5; they represent a time when they are not conscious of their 1.5 ethnic identity, but rather are in the process of developing a Korean American or local ethnic identity. The 1.5ers in the early part of their education observe a significant difference in the way immigrants are treated by Locals. Being singled out and ridiculed for their "FOBBY" dress and for not knowing how to speak English or speaking with an accent alienated them from other students and reinforced their desire to become more local or "American." Language is the distinguishing factor for Korean American 1.5ers at school. Their inability to communicate with non-Koreans and their Korean accent trigger taunts by their school peers. Such reactions to their language affect the 1.5ers' self-esteem. Travis recalls, "When I was younger, I was insecure about my surroundings and I became embarrassed [about my English]. It was around fifth or sixth grade that I became comfortable with others."

Although Korean 1.5ers eventually learn how to speak English with little to no accent, they have memories of feeling ashamed and embarrassed over their ethnicity. Even when there are other Korean-speaking students around, they remain embarrassed about their own "foreignness." Thus, the memory of being picked on and picked out as "different" remains. Consequently, 1.5ers befriend largely non–Korean Korean friends and Locals, who influence their understanding of what it means to be local and Korean American, not Korean Korean.

From elementary school to high school, the 1.5ers state that there were always Korean American students around, but Jenny, like other 1.5ers, states that it was in high school when she began to notice Korean Americans more. She explains, "They were too 'cliquey'; they only spoke Korean, hung with Koreans, and isolated themselves from others. We did not want to hang out with 'just' Koreans, particularly those at our schools. We wanted to blend in with the rest of the school and wanted to associate with the local students."

Korean Americans who immigrate during their high school years are bilingual with an accent but are not bicultural, and they cannot relate to local culture or to how it feels to grow up in Hawai'i. Thus, Korean 1.5ers treat them much like other first-generation Korean Americans. The stereotypes of the first generation are then applied to all Korean Americans by the 1.5ers. Because 1.5ers at this point in the process believe that all Korean Americans fit the stereotypes, they distance themselves from other Koreans in an attempt to fit in with the dominant group. Such beliefs hinder 1.5ers from fostering relationships with other Korean Americans.

LOCAL PEERS

To avoid being subject to the stereotypes of Korean Americans in Hawai'i, 1.5ers develop close relationships with local students. For Korean American 1.5ers, their preference at this point in the process is to hang out with non-Koreans. Because 1.5ers view all Koreans as the same, they do not see other 1.5 Korean Americans as similar to them and different from first-generationers. Instead, they look to non–Korean groups at school to befriend. Chris remembers, "I opted to hang out with the nons." Of the 1.5ers who opt to hang out with non-Koreans, some try to pass as members of the dominant group. For many 1.5ers in Hawai'i, their experiences at this time reinforce the image of Japanese Americans as the dominant group. Pat recalls wishing that he was Japanese. He states, "In intermediate and high school, I wanted to be [local] Japanese 'cause it's the respected race in Hawai'i. Because everyone's name was Japanese and Japanese were more Westernized. Chinese and Koreans were refugee-like."

The experiences of 1.5ers reflect the division between immigrants and Locals and the ethnic stratification that exists in Hawai'i. Pat's experience reflects not only the dichotomy between locals and immigrants, but the ethnic stratification that existed in his school. To be a part of the dominant "local" group, one had to be Japanese or a close friend of theirs.

The choice of friends is largely affected by the ethnic composition at the school. The 1.5ers who attend private schools have mostly non–Korean friends, largely because there are not a lot of Korean American students there. However, the 1.5ers at middle school also internalize stereotypes of Korean Americans, which affects their behavior and feelings toward other Korean Americans at school. Hilary states that most of her friends were Chinese, Japanese, and *haole*, but admits that her choice of friends had to do with her own stereotypes of Korean Americans, which hindered her interest in fostering relationships with other Koreans. At school, she says that she never spoke Korean. In fact, many of her classmates assumed that she was Chinese, she says. "I get mistaken for Chinese all the time." When 1.5ers are mistaken for other ethnic groups, they rarely correct the error, interpreting it as a "backhanded" compliment. It implies to 1.5ers that they are local, a part of the dominant group and no longer seen as the outsider.

Korean American 1.5ers' private school experience shields them from pidgin-speaking peers. However, 1.5ers who attend public schools experience pidgin-speaking Locals and are able to construct a positive sense of being local. These 1.5ers learn how to speak pidgin, appreciate and understand the different peoples and cultures

143

of Hawai'i, and take pride in belonging to Hawai'i's multicultural population. By belonging to and identifying with local culture, they are able to dismiss their Korean ethnicity. Particularly for those who attend public schools, it is easier for them to identify with being local than with being "American." Under their environmental conditions, it is more beneficial for them to appear local than *haole*. Chris states that he could never think of himself as "American" because to him, it means being white. He says, "Being white means assuming everyone is like you. Your impressions are everyone's impression. Even when there are five blacks present, you assume your perception of the world is shared by all. Whites see differences as quaint, as if the 'culture I'm used to is the standard we measure things against.'"

Chris's explanation of race relations in Hawai'i is influenced by his belief that race relations is a "white and people of color" issue. Because his observations of socioeconomic hierarchy have the Japanese at the top, he explains that the issues go beyond race. Due to the fact that his peers at school were non-Koreans, Chris says, "I think of myself as local first, Asian American second, and Korean last. I think it was when I went to Korea that I realized I wasn't like them. When I went to the mainland, I wasn't like [the other Asian Americans] either."

Dan also identified with Locals when he was in school. He says that at McKinley High School he befriended all local friends. In fact, he says that he was closer to his friends than to his own family. He appreciated his local friends taking him in, feeding him, having him sleep over at their homes, and meeting their families. He felt like his local friends were his brothers. Consequently, he adopted pidgin as his second language and switched from pidgin to English to Korean. Like Chris and Dan, other 1.5ers at this point in the process are exposed to pidgin-speaking Locals and embrace that culture in order to fit in and to disassociate themselves from being Korean. Under these conditions 1.5ers are able to express and construct a Korean American local identity.

For some Korean 1.5ers, having pidgin-speaking local friends is part of a greater appreciation for local culture. However, others interpret speaking pidgin as a sign of a lower social class and level of education. Such attitudes among Korean American 1.5ers cross class lines. It does not seem to matter which social class the 1.5ers come from, but rather whether they had close relationships with pidgin-speaking Locals when they were in school. Hilary states that she has never spoken pidgin. During high school, she really believed that pidgin speaking Locals were ignorant, poor, and/or uneducated.

Although the ethnicity of 1.5ers' friends affects whether they feel Korean, Korean American, or local, some state that the way schools segregate native English speakers from non-English speakers establishes the foundation for negative stereotypes. Mark states,

> *I think intermediate school is more of a factor. There is the age factor, like the English as a Second Language students stay with Korean and have less to do with Western culture. With ESL you isolate the Koreans and make them feel like they're less worthy in class. Like they are stupid, and the negative stuff weighs more on them. If you can go to the regular classes, you're likely to learn more and improve self-pride because you're forced to learn. ESL is backwards; they speak Korean or their own languages [in class].*

Korean American 1.5ers at this point in the process have not consciously embraced their 1.5 ethnic identity. Thus, their understanding of what it means to be Korean American and local stems from their experiences from the larger local community and peers at school. Some Korean Americans stay at this part of the process, remaining ashamed of their Koreanness and disassociating from their Korean ethnicity in favor of local or non–Korean Korean identity.

OTHER 1.5 ASIAN AMERICANS

The instinct to disassociate from Korean Americans is strong for 1.5ers. As they learn to negotiate their new ethnic options at school, they also seek out non–Korean friends who can relate to their experience. Because second-generation ethnics and Locals have a difficult time identifying with the immigrant experience, Korean American 1.5ers find that they can identify with other 1.5 Asian Americans. Other 1.5 Asian Americans share the experience of initially being an immigrant. Second, the 1.5 Asian Americans can relate to living and coping with first-generation parents and thus having to negotiate between two cultures. Finally, the other 1.5ers share the experience of feeling marginalized from the larger society. As a result, Korean American 1.5ers who developed close friendships with other 1.5 Asian Americans express a feeling of belonging to this generational identity early on. Travis states,

> At McKinley [High School] I had other 1.5 Cambodian, Vietnamese, and Laotian friends. There was racial tension [between the 1.5ers and Locals]. I got along with local Chinese and local Japanese; they were the more integrated group. There were no defined cliques, but I didn't get along with other local Samoan and Hawaiians. They were the dominant group who stuck together.

Because these Asian American friends were 1.5 generation, Travis felt that they could relate to his immigrant experiences of growing up in Hawai'i. The tension he felt with other local students had to do with his failure to establish close relationships with local students at that time.

A reason why Korean 1.5ers do not seek out other Korean American 1.5ers is their stereotypes of Korean Americans. They perceive Korean Americans in their schools to be "cliquey" and exclusive of other ethnic groups. The 1.5ers observe the Korean American cliques speaking primarily Korean outside of class and hanging out with only Koreans. Such images perpetuate their stereotypes of Korean Americans as an exclusive group. And even though there are other Korean American 1.5ers at school, the 1.5ers assume them to be like all Korean Americans. At this point of their process of becoming a 1.5er, Korean American 1.5ers have developed a sense of what it means to be Korean American and/or local. They do not have a clear understanding of what it means to be Korean American 1.5 generation. It is only when they interact with other Korean American 1.5ers that they discover the uniqueness of their generational identity. This will be discussed more in detail in Chapter 7.

Ashamed of Being Korean American

The ethnic stratification in Hawaiʻi makes it such that minorities experience alienation and shame of their ethnicity. Although second and subsequent generations have expressed feeling ashamed of their ethnic group,[2] they at least have the comfort of knowing that they are "American citizens" and English is their native tongue. The language barrier and the initial feeling of being an outsider are vivid memories for all 1.5ers. Aside from the inner frustration of learning a new language, 1.5ers are reminded and sometimes corrected by both Koreans and native English speakers of their language abilities. Hilary states that when she tells people that she was born in Korea, "They assume that my English is not as good as theirs and act differently toward me." Hilary's case marks how non-Koreans assume the power to critique those who are not American born and infer that they are not as fluent as native speakers. Although such criticisms ease as 1.5ers mature, the stereotypical images and anti-immigrant comments become embedded in their sense of identity as nonnative, foreigners, different from those born in the United States.

The need to conform to the dominant society, and even more important to "pass" as an intelligent second-generation or "American-born" Korean, is often the result of shame—specifically, frustration at not understanding English, being treated as "second-class citizens," and feeling alienated from the larger Hawaiian community. Even though 1.5ers may no longer experience these feelings, they still observe the difficulties of their parents and other immigrants.

A second reason why 1.5ers are ashamed of themselves are the stereotypes that depict Korean Americans in Hawai'i as materialistic, hot-tempered, pushy, and money hungry. However, the images of Korean bars and hostesses are the stereotypes that shame the 1.5ers the most. Although they are aware that the Korean hostess is a stereotype, jokes and comments from local friends and the island community reinforce their embarrassment and shame. Some may argue that stereotypes are images that should not be taken seriously, yet they have damaging effects on 1.5ers' sense of identity and self-worth. The 1.5ers are aware that they are not to take the stereotypes seriously, but at the same time, they cannot help but be disturbed by the depictions of Korean Americans.

Finally, the 1.5ers' experience at school also contributes to their shame in being Korean American. From elementary to high school, 1.5ers experience firsthand how it feels to be the outsider and observe how locals treat "FOBs." Having to attend special classes for students whose English is a second language marks them as different from the native speakers. Teachers remind them in their classes and in their graded papers that their grammar and overall writing style need improvement, but discount their problems by saying, "After all, English is not your first language." To avoid the stigma of being an immigrant, 1.5ers avoid contact with other Koreans who are overtly Korean or "FOBBY" and present themselves as Korean American or local. Thus, by disassociating with those who remind them and others of the existing stereotypes of Korean Americans, they are not perceived by the larger society as "typical" Koreans.

Embarrassment and shame of being Korean American is largely influenced by a combination of external forces and the interpretation of these images by 1.5ers themselves. The shame in part is due to 1.5ers not fully understanding their processual experience and how that has shaped their sense of ethnic identity. At this part of the process, 1.5ers disassociate from their Korean identity and affirm their Korean American or non–Korean Korean and local identity. The conditions at this time create a social environment where being Korean or an immigrant is not something they want to identify with. This process is a part of their discovery of becoming 1.5ers.

7

DISCOVERING 1.5
ETHNIC IDENTITY

Becoming 1.5 generation involves a process of discovery. Through the family, 1.5ers learn what it means to be Korean and Korean American, and from the community, the larger society, and their peers, they learn what it means to be Korean American/local. The external influences combined help 1.5ers maintain their bilingual and bicultural abilities. However, these factors alone do not account for a collective 1.5 ethnic identity. Korean American 1.5ers discover a sense of collective ethnic identity when they meet other 1.5ers who contradict the existing stereotypes of Korean Americans and have a shared experience of being child immigrants growing up in a non–immigrant-friendly community.

This chapter discusses what happens when 1.5ers discover what it means to be Korean American 1.5 generation. The case study of the Korean American Jaycees illustrates the growing number of 1.5ers who are actively participating in both the Korean American and local communities to reconstruct what it means to be Korean American today. The Korean Jaycees, a community organization composed of predominantly 1.5 generation and a few first-generation and second-generation Korean Americans, as well as some non-Koreans, is taking an active role in rethinking, renegotiating, and reconstructing how the different generations of Korean Americans are situated in the Korean American community and the larger Hawaiian society.

What Does It Mean to Be a 1.5er?

For the Korean American 1.5 generation, discovering ethnic identity is a new process. Growing up, in the beginning of the process of becoming 1.5, they are Korean, not Korean American, not 1.5ers, or even not local for that matter. They state and express their ethnicity as Korean. Though they can often pass as members of other Asian American ethnic groups, they state their true Korean ethnicity when asked. As they encounter the larger society, specifically their peers, they begin to question their ethnic identity. Although they state on forms and to those who may ask that they are "Korean," they do not feel "Korean Korean." Korean 1.5ers' conceptualization of what it means to be Korean stems from their stereotypes of and experiences with first-generation Korean Americans or Korean immigrants.

Growing up in Hawai'i, the options for ethnicity are greater for some and encumbering for others. Koreans in Korea clearly have one ethnic choice, and that is "Korean." In Hawai'i, 1.5ers realize that they have far more options than their ethnic counterparts in Korea. They learn in their homes how to express and construct their Korean and Korean American ethnicity. However, as they enter school, they experience alternative ethnic choices, such as Korean American and local, or even passing as Chinese American or Japanese American. But it is when they enter college or participate in Korean organizations catered to younger Korean Americans that they begin to meet other 1.5ers, rethink the prevailing stereotypes of Korean Americans in Hawai'i, and discover what it means to be Korean American 1.5 generation.

Meeting Other Korean American 1.5ers

The discovery of 1.5 ethnic identity has much to do with whether Korean Americans, in the process of becoming 1.5ers, meet other 1.5 Korean Americans. Some 1.5ers state that they had 1.5 Asian American friends, but it is not till they meet other 1.5 Korean Americans that they begin to understand what it means to be a Korean American 1.5er.

Korean American 1.5ers have various opportunities to meet other 1.5ers; however, it is not until they mature, enter college, join an organization composed mostly of 1.5ers, or experience Korean Americans outside of Hawai'i that they experience a critical mass of the 1.5 generation. Like other 1.5ers, Hilary began to see the advantages of her 1.5 ethnic identity when she returned home from college on the mainland. Her experiences with a different population of Asian Americans in general and Korean Americans in particular became the catalyst for rethinking her stereotypes of pidgin-speaking Locals and Korean Americans.

After high school, Hilary attended a prestigious private university close to Washington, D.C. In college, away from her parents and Hawai'i, she was able to express a different side of herself. The newfound freedom liberated Hilary to date and "party" with new friends. In college, she joined a Korean American social group "just to see what it was like" and found her stereotypes of first-generation Koreans backed up. Yet Hilary admits that her assessment of Korean Americans was biased, for they were mostly first generation. She did, however, meet other 1.5, second-, and third-generation Korean Americans who did not fit the stereotypes that she held. She said that for the most part, the Korean Americans she met initially did not know she was Korean, and she did not know that they were Korean. Hilary said that she just assumed that all Koreans were the same, not realizing that she herself is Korean and thinking she "isn't like other Koreans."

She began to realize that there are other Koreans who had the experience of living two lives, one with an immigrant family and the other with "Americans."

Hilary's experience of meeting other 1.5 Asian Americans and Korean Americans is similar to the experiences of other 1.5ers who went away to school. As they see positive representations of Korean American 1.5ers and Asian Americans, they begin to look at their own views about their ethnicity. Steve said that in college he began to take courses about different ethnic groups and realized how little he knew about Japanese and Chinese Americans. He then began to question how much of what he thought he knew about Korean Americans was true. For 1.5ers, learning about the sociohistorical experiences of other ethnic groups often serves as the catalyst for exploring their ethnicity.

For those who do not attend college, involvement in an organization with young Korean American adults is a common condition in which they begin to see and express their 1.5 ethnic identity. Joon states that before joining the Korean Jaycees, he interacted only with first-generation Korean Americans. He had never met so many Korean lawyers, doctors, accountants, and other professionals in one room. Exposure to the Korean Jaycees inspired Joon to go back to school to pursue a degree in business.

Experiencing other ethnic groups on campus also helped in the process of 1.5ers discovering their ethnic identity. Hilary said that she dated a Filipino American for the last 2 years in college. She was surprised to learn "how Filipinos on the mainland are different from those in Hawai'i." Her impressions of "'buk buks,'[1] dog eating, and FOBBY" Filipinos were modified after she entered college. Her experiences with other 1.5 Asian Americans made her more conscious of her own ethnic identity. As she began to look at her own stereotypes about other ethnic groups and local people, she reexamined how she had internalized stereotypes about Korean Americans.

For 1.5ers, the experience of meeting other 1.5 Korean Americans alters their views of Korean Americans. In college and in the States, 1.5ers are exposed to a more diverse population of Korean Americans. Their stereotypical images of Koreans are displaced when they meet other Koreans who speak without an accent but are also conversationally fluent in Korean. They realize that not all Korean Americans are materialistic and money hungry. Jenny states, "They're cool. They are not really Korean, they are more like us, more Americanized. . . . I did not even know they were Korean when I met them." This statement echoes the sentiments of other 1.5ers. The idea of not being able to tell that others are Korean supports the finding that 1.5ers when they were younger held rigid definitions of who Korean Americans were. Furthermore, college reinforces the importance of being bilingual and bicultural, and they no longer are ashamed of but take pride in their abilities. Because the 1.5ers now sound "American" and show no signs of being immigrants, speaking Korean is no longer a foreign trait, but a cultured and educated ability.

Another arena where Korean American 1.5ers meet other 1.5ers is organizations. In Los Angeles, there are a growing number of "1.5" organizations, yet there is no official organization in Hawai'i. However, the Korean Jaycees is an organization that is composed largely of Korean American 1.5ers in Hawai'i. By meeting and interacting with others like them, they become acquainted with a large number of 1.5ers who help dispel the stereotypes of Korean Americans in Hawai'i. These interactions create new images of Korean Americans as educated professionals who share the feelings of marginalization, shame, and eventual acceptance of their ethnic identity. With the Jaycees, 1.5ers are exposed not only to the 1.5 generation but to first-generation community members as well. As they come to terms with their own internalized prejudices against Korean Americans, they become more open to developing working relationships with first-generation Korean Americans.

Korean American 1.5ers discover the uniqueness of their 1.5 ethnic identity when they meet a large number of 1.5ers. They realize that they share four central experiences in being 1.5ers. First, a 1.5er sees that other 1.5ers share memories of Korea and of being an immigrant. They have a mutual experience of living with immigrant parents and of leading dichotomous lives between their home and the larger community. Second, they share the ability to switch between ethnic options in certain situations but acknowledge that when their 1.5 ethnic identity is revealed, they become marginalized from first-generation Korean Americans and non-Koreans. Third, they see that they are able to express both Korean and Korean American identities when they speak Konglish to other 1.5ers. Finally, they have a shared understanding of their sociocultural and personal experiences of growing up in Hawai'i. They mutually understand the feelings of shame and embarrassment but acknowledge the need to change their own and the larger Hawaiian society's impressions of Korean Americans in Hawai'i.

The feeling of having a shared sociocultural and personal experience creates a newfound acceptance of the 1.5 ethnic identity. A 1.5er realizes that he or she is not the only "demented" person, and the feelings experienced in the process of becoming a 1.5er were shared by other 1.5ers.

Discovering and Negotiating 1.5 Ethnic Identity

The position of the 1.5er is, in the beginning, an awkward place. As Koh (1994) states, 1.5ers face an identity crisis and are often in a position of limbo. However, this stage of "crisis" or limbo varies for 1.5ers. The vast majority of 1.5ers discover the positives of being 1.5 when they meet other 1.5ers who invalidate their internalized stereotypes of Korean Americans and use their ethnic options to their advantage. Jenny and Jane always knew that they were different from other ethnic and generational groups. Throughout elementary to high school, they felt as if they were in between and balancing two distinct worlds. Yet as they matured and met other 1.5ers, they began to accept and appreciate their Korean side, thus situationally switching their ethnic options with their family and friends.

By voicing their abilities as 1.5ers, they begin to understand the advantages of their generational and ethnic identities and to feel proud of their Korean heritage. One area where 1.5ers use their ethnicity to their advantage is in searching for jobs. Korean Americans 1.5ers highlight their bilingual abilities in their resumes and during interviews. They emphasize their abilities to work with a multi-ethnic population, and in particular with Korean Americans. For example, Jane, who is a social worker, states that whenever there is a Korean American client who cannot speak English, she is called in to talk to him or her. She says, "The majority of Korean people we see are immigrants, so they can't speak English. Although my Korean is not the best, I can converse with them and find out what we need to find out."

Jenny, on the other hand, did not highlight her bilingual abilities when she applied for an assistant manager position at a local business. However, after she got the job, she found her Korean to be useful. She says, "We get a lot of Korean small business owners and workers who come in here. They can't really speak English very well, and I guess they had a difficult time communicating with the other workers here. Now whenever they come in, they come looking for me. It's pretty cool." Other 1.5ers who work in tourism, banking, and law find their 1.5 abilities help them and their clients. They begin to realize that the process they went through while growing up has contributed to who they are. As a result, they are more comfortable with their status as 1.5ers and use their ethnic options in varying situations.

The process of becoming a 1.5er is a long and sometimes painful process. However, there are some who feel empowered by the process of discovery and strive to change the current stereotypes of Korean Americans. The next section discusses the Honolulu Korean Junior Chamber of Commerce to illustrate what Korean American 1.5ers are doing to construct a new image of Korean Americans in Hawai'i.

Honolulu Korean Junior Chamber of Commerce

The United States Jaycees is a volunteer organization of young men and women between the ages of 21 and 39. The main purpose of the organization is "to improve the quality of life and to develop the individual member to his or her full potential as a person, a concerned citizen and a leader."[2] The organization was started in 1920 as the Junior Chamber of Commerce with the purpose of helping young men in business. In 1965, the name was changed to "Jaycees" as the organization expanded into broader areas such as individual development and community service. Women attained full membership privileges nationwide in the early 1980s. The Honolulu Korean Junior Chamber of Commerce (Korean Jaycees) became an official member of the Junior Chamber of Commerce in October 1994, with a record-breaking 120 members in its first year. The Jaycees creed reads,[3]

> WE BELIEVE:
> That faith in God gives meaning and purpose to human life;
> That the brotherhood of man transcends the sovereignty of nations;

That economic justice can best be won by free
men through free enterprise;
That government should be of laws rather than
of men;
That earth's great treasure lies in human personality;
And that service to humanity is the best work of
life.

The Korean Jaycees state that in addition to promoting the Jaycees creed, their goal is "building a legacy for the future: through community partnerships." Moreover, their purpose is "to promote the Korean culture and heritage through community service while providing opportunities for leadership and personal growth." Thus, the overall goal of the Korean Jaycees is to educate the Korean American community and the larger Hawaiian community about Korean culture and heritage through community projects and services. In addition, the Jaycees officers and members state that they hope to achieve a better understanding of what it means to be Korean American.

The Jaycees currently have five officers—president, vice president of marketing, vice president of membership, treasurer, and secretary—and seven board members.[4] The board and the officers meet on the third Wednesday of each month, and the whole membership meets for a general meeting on the first Wednesday of each month to discuss goals and projects for the upcoming months.

The Korean Jaycees evolved through the joint efforts of four 1.5ers: Steve Kim, Hilary Kim, and brothers Trevor and Chris Chung. Steve sought the others' help to get the Jaycees started. From there, they collected the telephone numbers of their parents' friends' 1.5 and second-generation children and called them to see if they would be interested in starting a Korean Jaycees chapter. Steve said that in many ways, Hilary played a key part in recruiting members for the Jaycees because of her father's ties to the Korean American community. However, they all went through their parents' phone books and began calling. The referral approach worked, and in the first year, Steve became the president, with Hilary, Trevor, and Chris in officer positions. According to Steve, 95 percent of the members are Korean born but raised in the United States. They are bilingual and bicultural and identify themselves as being in between the first and second generations (1.5 generation). The rest are "a mixed bag of first and second generation."

Jaycees Membership

Presently, the Korean Jaycees are composed of approximately 90 percent Korean American 1.5 generation; 1 percent non-Koreans; 5 percent Korean born who immigrated in their late teens, are fluent in Korean, and speak English with a distinct Korean accent (first generation); and 4 percent born in the United States (second generation).[5] The group is not homogeneous by any means; there is a clear distinction between those Koreans who state that they are "Korean Korean" (first generation), "Korean and Korean American" (1.5 generation), and "Korean American" or "Korean local" (second generation). The "Korean Korean" (first generation) are those who immigrated in their late teens, speak with a noticeable Korean accent, feel more comfortable speaking Korean than English, and identify themselves as Korean. The "Korean and Korean American" (1.5 generation) are those who feel that they can identify with both cultures. This group was born in Korea but raised in Hawai'i, are able to converse in both English and Korean, and identify with being both Korean American and Korean, or somewhere "in between." The "Korean American" or "Korean local" (second generation) are those whose primary language is English and who are American born. They express feeling more American or local and do not identify with Korean culture. They do not speak or understand Korean except for a few words. Thus, within the Jaycees there are distinct generational groups that are openly recognized by the members. However, since the majority of the members are of the 1.5 generation, they serve as the medium and the bridge for the different generations.

Still, it is clear who socializes with whom outside of the Jaycees and the friendships that have developed based on generational and cultural lines. Those who self identify and are seen by others as "Korean Korean" associate with each other, and those who are Korean American/Korean local also socialize among themselves. The largest group of those who feel that they are in between, the 1.5ers, float between the two groups at different times but generally socialize with each other. The most noticeable difference between the groups is language. The second generation and 1.5ers speak English with no Korean accent, and some speak with a slight pidgin intonation. However, the 1.5ers are also able to converse in Korean with the first-generation members. The first generation have a thicker Korean accent when they speak English, speak Korean among themselves, and are able to read and write Korean. Some of the members even mention the way the "Korean" group dresses. Sean Chung commented during an interview, "Like the way you're dressed. You wear shorts . . . pretty casual. Some of the more Korean members would never come to lunch or outside dressed like that, like local. They have to have the makeup, wear designer clothes, and look a certain way. That's why they're more Korean than other members are."

Although dress and language are significant qualifiers, they are not the sole distinguishing characteristics of those who are seen as more Korean. The "more Korean" members maintain ties with the first-generation Korean American community. They either work for or with other first-generation Koreans or have direct contact with Korean nationals, which requires them to keep up with the language and cultural expressions. Furthermore, they identify themselves as being more Korean than Korean American or local. The recent experience of being an immigrant sets them apart from the 1.5 generation, who have had time to adapt and lose their Korean accent, and from the second-generation Korean Americans, who have not had to deal with the complications of being foreign born.

The Korean Jaycees nominate and elect new officers each year; thus, the group experiences leadership and membership changes annually. In the 1996–1997 year, the Korean Jaycees had over 200 members. It was by far the largest chapter in the nation, but the success was only on paper. Under the leadership of a past president, the group actively recruited members and signed up acquaintances or the children of their parents' friends. Only about 60 percent of the people actually paid for their membership; the other 40 percent signed up as a favor with no intention of ever really participating in the organization. Through fund-raising activities, the group was able to come up with the $50-per-member dues to register eighty members. In 1998, however, the officers decided that only those who invest in the Jaycees should participate, and they should be willing to pay their own dues except in the event of some unusual financial difficulties. So when the Jaycees asked for renewal of membership fees, those who did not initially pay did not want to pay the renewal fee. Thus, the organization experienced a drop of almost 40 percent in membership. Although this may seem like a large decrease, the number of people who are active in the organization remains constant; however, the retention of members is low. New members continue to join, but only a few from the original group have remained active in the Jaycees. Although all paying members are considered active, there are only a dozen members, the officers and the board, who consistently attend meetings and contribute to the organization.

Currently, the Korean Jaycees has ninety-eight members, of whom twelve are "active" forces. This core of a dozen members manages to organize events and recruit assistance when it is needed. Even among the core dozen, there are some who are more "into" the Jaycees than others. This has much to do with the time and flexibility allowed by their work schedules to devote time to Jaycees activities. For full-time professionals it is difficult to manage work, personal life, and the Jaycees. Because the organization requires much dedication with few rewards, the active members question their priorities; specifically, why do they invest so much of their time in an organization that is voluntary? Sarah, a Korean American who immigrated when she was a year old, but is not bilingual, states, "I do have a life outside of the Jaycees. I have to remind myself that this is a volunteer organization and I am volunteering."[6]

There are some obvious reasons why people drop out. The Jaycees is a voluntary organization, and a new one. The twelve core members state that there are three main reasons for joining the Korean Jaycees: to gain experience in community work and business, to help the Korean American community, and because it looks good on their resumes. With regard to the first reason, some feel that it has been a good experience while others feel it is not what they expected. It is those who enter to help the Korean American community who remain with the Jaycees. But even among this group there are those who are willing to remain until the work in the community is finished, whereas others feel that the needs are endless and unfulfilling. The members who seek to contribute to the Korean American community state that their focus is on the current state of the community, which includes the needs of mostly the first generation. The 1.5 generation members in the Jaycees feel that there is currently a void and a misrepresentation of who Korean Americans are in Hawai'i.

Jaycees' Choices of Activities and Community Functions

The members of the Jaycees are different from the those of first-generation Korean American community organizations, such as the United Korean Society. Currently, there are no second-generation Korean American community organizations in Hawai'i; thus, the Jaycees feel that the larger society's impressions of Korean Americans have been shaped by the first generation. They state that their interests lie not only in the Korean American community but in how they can present themselves and offer their services to both the Korean and local communities. As a result, they participate in events such as a citizenship drive, which caters to Koreans but welcomes all immigrants filing for citizenship; golf tournaments; Korean sumo wrestling; Korean traditional chamber music; Korean sports contests; and other Korean-focused events to make Korean Americans more visible in the community.

The Jaycees believe that they play an important role in these various activities. First, they are given an opportunity to address both Korean and local television audiences. They feel that by participating in Korean and local community functions, they are sending the message to the largely Korean audiences of the Korean television channels that the younger generations are interested in Korean American community affairs. Via the local television broadcast, the 1.5ers are able to relay a new impression to the larger Hawaiian society. By showing images of Korean Americans as community-oriented, articulate professionals, they help to debunk the existing stereotypes of Korean Americans. Although there are first-generation Korean Americans who are bilingual and are able to provide the same information to the general public, the 1.5ers' presence sends a different message. What is significantly different about the 1.5ers is that to the general Hawaiian community, Korean Americans are no longer presented as immigrants with distinct Korean accents. The 1.5ers are fluent in English, are articulate, are involved in Hawai'i and not only Korean businesses and community activities, and are inclusive of all ethnic groups in their community activities. The Jaycees stress that although they are the Korean Jaycees, they have a small number of non-Korean members.

Thus, the Jaycees' participation in these types of events sends out messages to three different groups. To the Korean American first-generation community, the message, as Sean Chung states, is that "the Korean Jaycees is a group comprised mostly of 1.5ers" who have a vested interest and are committed to enhancing and presenting a holistic image of Koreans in Hawai'i. The other two groups are the second-generation Korean Americans and the larger local community, who become more aware of Korean Americans' role in facilitating community activities. In addition, the Jaycees hope that their inclusion of all Koreans and other ethnic groups, not just first-generation Koreans, can serve to eliminate the stereotypical image of Koreans as exclusive of others and unapproachable. They hope to create a new image of Korean Americans as articulate, community oriented, and open to all of Hawai'i's ethnic groups. This effort seeks to present Korean Americans as a community-based and community-focused group rather than one that is insular and polarized.

In attempting to present a new image of Korean Americans, the Jaycees have participated in various community activities. One of the most successful events is the Aloha Parade. The Korean Jaycees have won the Mayor's Award for the best nonprofit organization float for several years. The parade is significant for the Jaycees because the process of getting their float together includes the work of the Korean American community and the larger local community. Andy Shim states that in the past, the Jaycees had to reach out to both the Korean American and local communities for financial support. Without the donations of community businesses, they could not get the float up and going. He says that as they were ready to move the float into the parade, the truck pulling the float broke down. The Jaycees had to call a tow truck to pull their float in the parade. Andy and Sean feel that the tow truck pulling the Korean Jaycees float is symbolic of the current relationship of the Korean American community and the larger local community: Sometimes "you need the help of others to get you going." Such sentiments are something the Jaycees hope to convey to both the Korean American and local communities. By seeking and accepting assistance, the Jaycees hope to send the message that they want to work with other communities.

Another event that the Jaycees have participated in since 1996 is the U.S. citizenship drive. They say that there are Korean Americans who do not know how to fill out the application for citizenship or understand the basic process of gaining citizenship. Thus, the Jaycees have taken an active role in helping the Korean immigrant community. Though the focus is to help the Korean community, the Jaycees have also invited other immigrants to attend the citizenship drive. The main problem, however, is that while the Jaycees have interpreters for the Korean American applying for citizenship, they do not offer the same service for other ethnic groups. Jodie states that in the future, it may be a good idea to work with other ethnic groups to hold a collective citizenship drive so that translation services can be provided for all applicants.

These are just a few of the activities that the Jaycees participate in every year. They also organize activities for just the Korean American community. They feel that it is important to let the Korean American community know that the newer generation of Korean Americans are invested in the community and its people. In December 1997, the Jaycees gathered members and nonmembers to sing Christmas carols at the Korean convalescent home. Most of the songs were in English, but they sang Korean Christmas carols as well. The aging Korean audience smiled and sang along when the carolers sang in Korean.

The Korean Jaycees, with its large 1.5 membership, is able to communicate with various generations and ethnic groups and serves as the bridge to transform the Korean American community as the larger society knows it into the mainstream "local" and Korean American communities. They strive to become an integral part of the total Hawaiian community while simultaneously expressing their unique culture. Although this is one method by which the 1.5ers bridge the first-generation, second-generation, and local communities, Jaycees leaders face challenges as *Korean American* Jaycees.

There are two school of thought among Jaycees members. The first-generation members feel that the goal and focus of the organization is to serve the Korean American community by emphasizing Korean culture, ancestry, community, and people. The 1.5 generation in the Jaycees state that although the focus on the Korean American community is important, there is a need to transform the image of Korean Americans in Hawai'i. To do this, this group feels that they must make themselves more visible to the community at large and not limit their services to Koreans. These perspectives are not dissimilar to those of first-generation Koreans; there are those who seek to interact only with Korean organizations and businesses, and others who want to merge with the larger community. The problem stems from the fact that Korean Americans in Hawai'i are not a homogeneous group. As Hilary states, "The [first-generation] Korean American community is not cohesive; they have their own social groups and churches" and do not get along with each other.[7] The first generation have difficulty coming to a consensus, so it is not surprising that their children are faced with similar factions in their 1.5 organization.

The 1.5ers who wish to assimilate with the mainstream local community want to distance themselves from the "negative" image of Korean Americans—the stereotypes that Koreans are only out for themselves, are hard to get along with, and are self-motivated and exclusive of other ethnic groups. Although they wish to distance themselves from the stereotypes, they initially express the desire to distance themselves from the first-generation community. However, this is an unrealistic objective since 1.5ers are constantly exposed to and in situations where they have to interact with other Korean Americans. Even if they do not work or socialize with first-generation Koreans, they cannot help but associate with them. The 1.5ers in Hawai'i voluntarily or involuntarily interact with the first generation and the Korean American community because their parents are part of it. In addition, first-generation Koreans who are not in the business professions still shop at Korean markets, attend Korean churches, and have Korean friends.

Korean Jaycees members are aware of this involvement, and as a community-focused organization that has an ethnic label attached to it, they and the organization cannot help but be associated with first-generation Korean Americans. Despite this association, the first-generationers still question whether the Jaycees are a "Korean" organization. Mr. Ho, a first-generation taxi driver, mentions, "Korean people are hard to get through. They appear to be closed and unwilling to open up, but once you get in, you're accepted and they treat you like family." On both the personal and professional levels, this is the case with first-generation Koreans and to some extent the 1.5 generation. The Jaycees have the official "Korean" title that helps identify them, but they do not receive support or endorsement from the first generation. The 1.5ers have to prove themselves and the organization as being dedicated to the Korean American community and people. As Sean points out, "You have to network with both Korean and the [local/American] community to have legitimacy [as the linking bridge between cultures]."

Korean Jaycees' Relationship with First-Generation Korean Americans

Sean states that despite the various efforts made by the Korean Jaycees in the past year, the first-generation community leaders have not fully accepted the Korean Jaycees, and more specifically the 1.5ers, as contributing equals. One main problem facing the 1.5ers is language. Although 1.5ers speak conversational Korean, they are unable to communicate and exchange ideas with the first generation on political and social issues. Mark, a 24-year-old 1.5er, states that members of the United Korean Society have been asking him about his plans, whether he would run for [UKS] president. He says, "I'm not ready for it. I do not want to offend any Koreans because I cannot speak Korean." When asked if he is conversationally fluent, he replies,

169

> *Yeah, but with the [UKS] organization, I would have to make presentations and speeches, and I can't do that with just conversational Korean. I would have to learn a lot more to do that. The United Korean Society is a first-generation organization. They don't like change. They figure, if it's not broken then don't fix it. I think it has a lot to do with age. They fear [change]; younger people fear [change] less.*

The UKS inquisition into Mark's plans is targeted toward the future. With an organization that is first-generation run, the idea of a 24-year-old president is not realistic. Rather, the UKS members are starting to think about who will continue running the organization in the future. In addition, with the community being led by first-generation immigrants, 1.5ers believe that when they begin to participate in community affairs as adults, they are not taken seriously and are seen merely as "children" of the leaders in the community. As a result of the first generation's Confucian belief system, the elders consider themselves the wise decision makers, with the younger generations there to learn from their wisdom and experience.

Korean Jaycees' Relationship with Korean Americans and the Local Community

Second-generation Korean Americans share the difficulties of interacting with first-generation Korean Americans, and in some ways feel more alienated than the 1.5ers. Because the second generation are American born, first-generation Koreans discount their Americanized or local behavior and do not expect them, as they may 1.5ers, to speak or participate in Korean activities. In addition, because first-generation organizations conduct their meetings and activities in Korean, second-generation Korean Americans have a difficult time understanding the proceedings. Furthermore, the traditional Korean social cues of the first generation are foreign to the "Americanized" second generation. Thus, the number of second-generation organization members has thus far been small. The name Korean Jaycees deters some second-generation Korean Americans from joining. They assume that the Jaycees, like other Korean organizations, are run by the first generation. However, those few second-generation Korean Americans who participate find the experience to be positive. Jodie, a second-generation Korean American, states that she joined the Korean Jaycees because she became curious about Korean Americans after meeting non-first-generation Korean Americans in college. When she joined the Jaycees, she met other Korean Americans but was surprised to find that most of them were not born in the United States. Jodie states,

> *The people in the Jaycees are cool. They are in many ways like us [the second generation]. Initially, I thought that most of them were born in the U.S., but when I heard them speaking to other first-generation Koreans [with ease], I was really impressed. It made me change my views about Koreans who aren't American born.*

Jodie stresses how her impressions of Korean Americans have changed since she joined the Jaycees. She realized that not all Koreans are alike and that there are generational differences among them. But more important, Jodie has changed her own outlook toward herself as a Korean American. She feels that the Jaycees were able to open her eyes to how her generation can contribute to and possibly change the future of Koreans in Hawai'i.

Case Studies of 1.5
Generation Jaycees Members

STEVE PARK, JAYCEES PRESIDENT

Personal History:
Immigration, Family, and Education

Steve Park, a 27-year-old, immigrated to Hawai'i with his parents in 1974, when he was 5 years old. His father worked as a machine operator in Korea and his mother was a nurse. His father had a year of college and his mom went to nursing school. Steve says that his parents' meeting was romantic "My dad's truck overturned and my mom ended up as his nurse, so they fell in love. She went to Germany for awhile, but when she returned they married." When he was 2 years old, his parents left Steve with his paternal grandmother and headed for Washington, D.C. On their way to D.C., they stopped in Hawai'i and ran out of money, so they remained. His mom was introduced to a care home, and she has been working there ever since. After 3 years Steve joined his parents in Hawai'i, and a year later his sister, Jenny, was born there.

When they first arrived in Hawai'i, his mother worked as a nurse, and his father went to Kapiolani Community College and learned welding. Mr. Kim was an ironworker for 10 years and worked for E.K. Hernandez for 3 years. He then left for Seattle to work with Boeing for a few months, but hated the weather and returned to Hawai'i. He has driven a cab (for a Korean-owned cab company) for the past 15 years.

After they settled in Hawai'i, his mom arranged a marriage for her female cousin in Korea with a divorced Korean American man with two children in Hawai'i. Mrs. Kim saw it as a method to bring her family over to the United States. Her cousin and the man married but divorced after 5 years. About that time, Mrs. Kim sponsored her brothers to Hawai'i, but her parents decided to stay in Korea.

Growing up, Steve attended Damien, a private high school for boys. He states that his parents "worked their butts off so that I could receive the best education." He went on to a private university in the East Coast. He says that it was in college that he began to reevaluate his Korean ethnicity. He saw how active Asian Americans were in the continental United States, and sensed that Asian Americans were a determined and proud group. He participated in an Asian American fraternity, where he met Asian American men from all ethnic groups who did not speak pidgin English or "FOBBY."

Ethnic Options and
1.5 Generation Ethnic Identity

Steve says that growing up he never felt comfortable with his ethnicity. He believed that his first-generation parents and relatives could not understand how he felt growing up in Hawai'i. Yet he also believed that his second-generation Korean American friends or non-Korean friends neither understood nor shared in his experience of being a 1.5er. He says that people like him, the "1.5[er]s," are the "demented" generation. He explains, "When I said that the 1.5 [generation] were demented, I mean that we are confused. When I'm with first- or second-generation Koreans, I don't feel like I belong. I'm most comfortable with those who are like me, the 1.5ers. When I'm with my local friends, I don't talk about cultural stuff."

Steve's use of the word *demented* refers to his confusion and discomfort with being in-between or being a marginal Korean American. The feeling of anomie or helplessness was compounded by his feeling of not being understood and thus demented. He states that growing up, all of his friends were local Chinese, Japanese, and Caucasians. Yet it was not until he met other 1.5ers that he felt as if he belonged and was understood. Steve's sense that Korean Americans from his generation are demented has influenced the way he views his Korean ethnicity. He says,

> *I used to be embarrassed about being Korean. I didn't want people to know I was Korean.*

> *When I'm with [my local friends], I still want to assimilate and don't want to be Korean. With local friends, we talk about stuff, not cultural stuff. We speak pidgin, talk about old-time days, people we know in high school. I'm just being myself.*

Steve discussed how feeling embarrassed about his Korean ethnicity led him to find another ethnic option of which he could be proud. Because when he was growing up all of his close friends were local, he also identified as local. He was able to converse in pidgin, although at home he spoke Korean. Yet when he was with his friends, he did not have to think about his confusion and "dementia," but just be local. When asked if being local is really who he is, he replied, "Well, I tried to hide being local in [college]. I tried to be straight nose, tried to enunciate words and all. When I got back, I spoke proper English, fooling myself of thinking that's who I am." Though Steve's response did not clearly answer the question, he makes some interesting points about his choice of ethnic expression. Whereas in high school and with his local friends he expressed his local side by speaking pidgin and being "more open," in college he tried to present a different side to his peers in the East Coast. In college, he spoke standard English and attempted to blend in with the dominant group. What is interesting about his ethnic choices is that he was able to express local and "American" ethnicities in the different situations. In Hawai'i, speaking pidgin has its advantages since it is a marker of being local and therefore being part of the larger island community. However, as Steve found out, speaking pidgin in the continental United States is not received in the same light; therefore, he had to reconstruct how he presented himself to others by speaking standard English. Yet Steve's uneasy feeling had to do with his own generational consciousness. He was always aware that he was not truly local or Korean, like his parents. Thus, he felt that although he could pass with either group, he really did not belong to either.

He states that in high school, the opportunities to speak pidgin were common, for his social interactions occurred with his local friends, who switched from pidgin to standard English. The collective expression of a local identity solidified his feelings of being local. However, in college he did not have the opportunity to express his local identity. He began to speak only standard English in an attempt to sound "more intelligent." Yet with both local and "American" groups, he never felt as if he totally belonged. He says that he did not know that he did not belong, for when he was with his local friends he was content, and when he was with his college friends he was also content. However, he felt as if his friends could not understand what it was like to be someone who was constantly in between ethnic groups, someone who could switch from pidgin to English to Korean as the situation warranted. He said that others could not really understand his experience as a Korean 1.5er, except for other 1.5ers, for they never had to deal with the different generational and ethnic options. He states, "I never knew it before [spending time with the Jaycees], but I feel most comfortable with people my age and people like myself. Like you, a 1.5[er]. I don't have to practice or [act with] anything. [The 1.5ers are] people who can empathize with you [and your experience]." Though Steve seemed to assimilate with both local and American cultures, he says that although "I tried to fit in and assimilate, I never felt like I really belonged until [I formed the Jaycees and met other 1.5ers]."

SEAN CHUNG, JAYCEES PRESIDENT

Personal History:
Immigration, Family, and Education

Sean Chung, a 29-year-old, immigrated to Hawai'i when he was 5 years old, in 1974. In Korea, Sean's parents separated, and his mother decided to leave for the United

States and start a new life. Mrs. Chung's sister, who was married to a Korean American military man, sponsored her to Hawai'i. For financial reasons, she immigrated alone and left Sean to live with his maternal aunts until she was settled. A year later, she petitioned for Sean and his brother Bob, who was 7 at the time, to join her. She also tried to petition for their father; however, shortly after they moved to Hawai'i Mr. Chung was diagnosed with lung cancer, and he died a year later, when Sean was 8 years old. That same year, Mrs. Chung successfully petitioned her brother, who was working in Taiwan, to join her.

Sean, his family, and his uncle rented a house in Kāhala and lived together. Sean and his brother went to elementary school in Kāhala and had mostly haole friends. He says that his friends in the neighborhood were like the Leave It to Beaver family, and he was often ashamed of his non–English-speaking mom and uncle. He wanted his family to be like those in the neighborhood. When he was in intermediate school, his family ran into some financial problems and they had to move to Mōili'ili. He went to Washington Intermediate School, where mostly local kids attended. He began to cut school because he did not take education seriously. As a result, his mom sent Sean and his brother to California for the summer to "straighten him out," but afterward his uncle said that he could not deal with him. His mom had heard about a boarding school in South Carolina, so for the next school year he and his brother were sent there. They stayed in a dorm with some college students, which contributed to their interest in college. They did well in school, and for his final year in high school he went to Mid-Pacific Institute. He says that he was fortunate to have gone to a private school because he feels that the environment really does affect how well you do and on what you focus your energies. He did not do as well in Mid-Pac but still did well enough to get into a private university in California.

Ethnic Options and 1.5 Ethnic Identity

In college, Sean began to explore his Korean American side. He says in his first year he hung out with a group of students from Hawai'i and Caucasian students. In the second year, however, "I found my niche by joining the Korean clubs and meeting other 1.5 and second-generation Korean Americans." He felt more comfortable with them because he felt like he belonged. He also joined a Korean church and began to speak Korean more often, and to eat and hang out with Korean Americans. He says that his early embarrassment and shame of being Korean diminished as he met more educated and professional Korean Americans. He says that he was at one time, "embarrassed of the Korean smells in his house. Now when I smell kimchee, it's comforting. A few years ago, I would have found the smell offensive."

Sean now sees the advantages of being bilingual and bicultural. He states that as the Jaycees president, he finds himself in situations where he has to be Korean, local, or American. He says that regardless of whom or which community organization he is addressing, he finds himself adapting to the situation. He is able to discuss Korean American community matters with first-generation Korean Americans and an hour later go to a non-Korean function and discuss necessary community matters. He says that now, instead of being embarrassed, he sees the importance of being a Korean American 1.5er.

Reasons for Starting and Joining the Korean Jaycees

Steve says that when he returned from college, he wanted to form an organization where 1.5 and newer generations of Asian Americans would get together and work in the community. Steve had a few friends in the Chinese Jaycees, so he approached them about joining. To his surprise, they encouraged him to start a Korean Jaycees chapter. Steve thought that starting such an organization might be an opportunity to meet other "demented" people like himself. He said that he was always curious about other Korean Americans who were bicultural and bilingual (1.5ers) and felt like they did not belong. He wondered if their experience was similar to his, if they felt as confused and lost about their ethnicity as he did. The Jaycees seemed to reach out to professionals who wanted to work with and for the community. Moreover, a Korean Jaycees organization could also help put Korean Americans "on the map" in Hawai'i.

Sean states the he joined the Korean Jaycees a year after its inception. He says that he joined for two reasons: because Steve had called him and asked him to join and because he wanted to continue the type of relationships he had with Korean Americans in California. He also liked the idea of meeting other professional Korean Americans who wanted to do philanthropic work for the Korean American community. He did not really know what the generational composition was going to be, but he assumed that most of the members would be Korean American. He says that he could have just as easily joined the Hawai'i Chamber of Commerce to do community work, but by joining the Korean Jaycees he believed he could give something to the Korean people in Hawai'i and learn something about his culture at the same time. Sean says that he did not plan to be president. After joining 4 years ago, he has served on the board and as an officer. However, when the election was approaching, no one in the organization wanted to be president. Sean states that he ran by default. He did not want the organization to disappear, and at the same time, he thought he could learn a lot from the position.

Bridging the Communities

Steve says that his intent was not to have an organization with predominantly 1.5ers, but he is glad that he was able to attract so many people like himself. He says that a few first- and second-generation members signed up, but that for the most part, the newly formed Jaycees chapter seemed to attract the 1.5 generation. Steve says that this is largely due to the various organizations that are geared toward first-generation Korean Americans. He says that the first generation usually wants to participate in a first generation–run organization, and they see the Korean Jaycees a product of the ilchom ose. Second, the first generation already has the established United Korean Society, in which the larger part of the membership are first generation. Finally, because Korean Jaycees meetings are conducted in English, first-generation Korean Americans who are not comfortable with English or are not fluent find the Korean Jaycees foreign to them.

The Korean Jaycees also recruited a few second-generation Koreans. Steve found that for the second generation, Korean culture and Korean American community affairs did not seem to be the primary interest. They wanted to join organizations that were more inclusive of others and not so polarized. Because of the second generation's assimilation into the local culture, they tend to participate in larger-community activities. The Korean Jaycees leaders felt that their organization was a medium for the second generation, an organization where they could pursue their Korean culture and work on behalf of the Korean American and Hawai'i communities.

Though the Korean Jaycees attracts mostly the 1.5 generation, they are trying to reach the second as well. Steve says that although 1.5ers have the benefit of being bicultural and bilingual, which helps in working with the Korean American community, the reasons 1.5ers join vary. Steve feels that it is largely due to the fact that their parents' phone books, which they used as a reference, listed predominantly 1.5 generation children between the ages of 21 and 39. The first-generation Korean Americans tend to be too old to join the Jaycees, and the second generation, victims of Korean American stereotypes, are wary of joining the organization.

To promote the Korean Jaycees and its 1.5 generation members, Steve feels that their best asset is the ability of the 1.5 generation to fulfill both the Korean Jaycees' and the general Jaycees' goals by serving as mediator, translator, and ambassador for Korean Americans in Hawai'i. Although the first-generation organizations have not embraced this new group, the Jaycees are actively working in the community to demonstrate their ability to forge a relationship between Korean Americans and the larger community. They have worked with different chapters of the Jaycees encompassing a diverse ethnic population and with the Korean Consulate to discuss the future of Korean communities. In addition, the Jaycees have sought out the assistance of non–Korean community members in Korean Jaycee–sponsored events to demonstrate a new, inclusive Korean American organization. Sean, whose beliefs are similar to Steve's, says,

> We as 1.5[er]s can understand the needs of the Korean American community, but at the same time understand how to deal with the American culture. Our method of communicating with non-Koreans is more likely to bridge the relationship with the [Korean] community and the others [non-Korean American community]. But the first generation still will not let go of the control and still treat us like children.

Problems Dealing with First-Generation Korean Americans Outside of the Jaycees

Sean explains that it is difficult to conduct business the Korean way, and there is a need to begin exploring business dealings beyond just those with Koreans. Sean says that because the first generation treat 1.5ers like children or inferiors, some 1.5ers have developed a propensity to avoid professional and social relationships with them. Steve confirms Sean's observations and states,

> *With my job [at a bank], there are times that I have to work with first-generation Koreans, but it is not my choice. I end up with them because of my [Korean] speaking abilities.*
>
> *The first-generation merchants demand [a lot from the] 1.5 generation. They rely on us to speak Korean, demand special treatment, they are pushy, but don't deal with locals [like that]. They expect that bilingual [1.5ers] have an obligation as educated Koreans to do this. They are more demanding and expecting. They brush it off on us, and it infuriates me.*
>
> *Koreans don't mention* Ghe *to anyone; they hide it. But to me, they say, "you're Korean so I can tell you this." They have the attitude of "you owe us this service."*[8]

Another thing that bothers Steve is that Korean customers often ask him to do illegal things. He says that they tell him of illegal activities they are involved in and ask him to do ethically questionable things. For Steve, this perpetuates the stereotypical images of Koreans.

Although 1.5ers express resentment toward their first-generation counterparts, interaction with them is often inevitable. For example, Steve states that though he would prefer to work with the general population, his ability to converse in Korean puts him in a position where he has to work with first-generation Koreans. He states that most of his clients are in fact non–Korean Americans, because of the location of his office. He adds, however, that any Korean American merchant who enters the bank is directed to him by other workers. Thus, whether a 1.5er is directly involved in the Korean American community or works in a predominantly mainstream business, his or her bilingualism and biculturalism is acknowledged and used in business when necessary. Some hide their bilingual ability, and Steve states that although it is "annoying" at times, it is also beneficial for him and the customers. Those who want to become active members in the Korean American community have little choice but to interact with the first generation.

Some 1.5ers state that as a result of dealing with the first generation, they have a better understanding of this group. Sean says that serving as president of the Jaycees has given him a different impression of first-generation Korean Americans. He states,

> I now know why the [first-generation] Korean American community is the way they are. They are trying to find their own recognition. I mean, they have to forgo their own goal and dreams for their children. I know of [one parent] who had dreams of being a lawyer, but didn't pursue his education. He says now, it's up to our generation to fulfill his dreams. The first-generation parents work hard so they can make a good future for their kids, so they can be included in their kids' lives.

Sean states that in the past, he did not want to deal with the first generation due to his internalized stereotypes about them. Today, however, he feels that it is necessary to work with the first generation, who have given up for the emerging generation. He states that although the Jaycees want to go "mainstream" right away, it is important to work with the first generation first to produce a unified Korean American community.

The feelings of embarrassment and shame transform when 1.5ers, as young adults, participate in organizations that focus on Korean American issues and when 1.5ers begin to interact with other Korean Americans. Sean states, "I didn't like being Korean at one time, but instead of ignoring it, I decided that I wanted to change that perception so I wouldn't feel bad about being Korean."

The 1.5ers, through a process of interacting with Korean and non–Korean American community organizations, have learned to negotiate their unique ethnic options. Although they resent the negative stereotypical images perpetuated by the larger society, they take pride in their first-generation parents' work and family ethics. Their ethnicity clearly marks them as Korean, but they do not feel a part of the first-generation Korean American community. At Korean American community activities, the first-generation leaders continue to treat them as children; thus, the 1.5ers feel that they do not have respect or an equal voice in community matters. In addition, although they do not identify as second generation, they feel that they can pass and to some extent be included in second-generation activities. They can easily contribute to general local community functions, frequented by second-, third-, and fourth-generation Korean Americans and non–Korean Americans, yet they are not able to express their unique 1.5 ethnic identity at these activities. Instead, they switch to their "American" or "local" ethnic option. The 1.5ers seek a way to find a balance where they can continue to express their unique ethnic and generational identity. Still, the feeling of belonging to a community did not exist for the 1.5 generation until they met other Korean American 1.5ers as adults and thus became conscious of their 1.5 ethnic identity.

The process of becoming a 1.5er is influenced by several external factors; however, it is not until 1.5ers meet other 1.5ers that they have an understanding of what it means to be Korean American 1.5. The 1.5ers' shared understanding of their sociocultural experiences validates their separate and unique ethnic identity. For some, discovering what it means to be a 1.5er serves as a catalyst to work in Korean American and local communities to shatter the stereotypes of Korean Americans and to present a new image of the Korean American community.

8

WHAT DO THE 1.5 GENERATION KOREAN AMERICANS TELL US?

When I began this research, my goal was to examine the unique social characteristics and cultural expressions of the Korean American 1.5 generation, and what it means to be Korean American in Hawai'i. I wanted to understand the process by which Korean Americans express and construct a 1.5 generation ethnic identity and determine if in fact the sociocultural and historical experiences of Korean American 1.5ers are sociologically significant.

The purpose of this study was to examine the process of discovering a 1.5 generation identity. Specifically, at what point in their resocialization do Korean Americans transfer their immigrant first-generation status to 1.5 generation status? What are the major influences that contribute to the process of shaping Korean American 1.5 identity? Moreover, how and under what conditions do these Korean Americans express, construct, and become conscious of their 1.5 identity?

The *ilchom ose*, or 1.5 generation, are sociologically and culturally unique. However, what is clear about this group is that, like first- or second-generation Korean Americans, the 1.5 generation are not a homogeneous group but vary depending on such factors as geography, social class, gender, and sexuality.

The 1.5 generation are unique in that they share the basic characteristics of bilingualism and biculturalism and the ability to cross generational and ethnic lines. However, the way in which the 1.5 generation construct their generational and ethnic identity has much to do with where they live and the community that surrounds them. Hawai'i, often seen as a multicultural paradise, provides a different social space for Korean immigrants to settle in. With the majority of the population being of Asian descent, it may appear that for Asian Americans, Hawai'i provides an ideal racial climate. However, the reality of Hawai'i is that race relations take on a different face than in the continental United States. Although Asian Americans do not have to deal with living in a visibly white society, there is a racial hierarchy that stems from colonization and the plantation era. Much like the legacy of slavery and its plantation roots, Hawai'i's plantation history has established a racial class system that puts Caucasians at the top and Native Hawaiians at the bottom. The Chinese, Japanese, and Koreans fall in the middle of the hierarchy. Thus, contemporary Hawai'i has not overcome the stratification that existed during plantation-era Hawai'i. What makes Hawai'i significantly different from the continental United States is the presence of local culture and identity. Although the term *local* was historically used to demarcate plantation workers from the white military and plantation owners, it has found a sociopolitical space in Hawai'i that provides some sense of legitimacy for those who can claim local status. Consequently, Korean Americans and other people of Asian decent can be part a group that is seen to have a stake and a history in Hawai'i.

The legacy of the plantation era is still highly visible in many facets of Hawai'i's communities. The one factor that continues to separate people is social class. Middle-class Korean Americans tend to embrace the capitalistic notion of social mobility and success, whereas working-class Korean Americans are more invested in making ends meet, participating in local culture, and making Hawai'i a home. Surprisingly, middle-class Korean American 1.5ers in this study expressed more pride in being Korean than the working-class Korean Americans. This is, in large part, due to the access to cultural capital and resources available to the middle class. Middle-class 1.5ers are more likely to attend Korean language schools in Hawai'i, study abroad in Korea, participate in cultural events with their parents and friends, and learn more about the history of Korea and its rich culture from their parents. Working-class Korean Americans, on the other hand, are more likely to be victims of Korean stereotypes and have limited opportunities for cultural discourse with their parents, who also have had little exposure to the arts or Korean history. Working-class 1.5ers express more pride in being local than in being Korean. Not having class clout in the Korean community, they are able to find a sense of community and identity with locals, who also embrace working-class culture.

Solidarity among community members is something that most people look for, and for women and the gay, lesbian, bisexual, and transgender (GLBT) community, this is also the case. Half of my respondents were women, but I had only one respondent who was openly gay. For women, the issues revolve around the stereotypes that exist in Hawai'i. Despite the increasing number of Korean 1.5 women in professional fields, they have a hard time shedding the image that Korean women in Hawai'i have associations with the hostess bar industry. This creates friction and obstacles for many Korean 1.5 women, who feel that the stereotype delegitimizes them as women and creates a hostile environment in which they feel accosted by men who perceive them to be hostesses. Though many working-class and middle-class women assert that they have nothing personal against women who work in the bars, the perpetuation of the stereotype that this is the general occupation of Korean women upsets them.

Family obligations are something that also haunts many Korean American women. Although some men also express a loss of childhood, taking care of household functions and siblings is gendered. Women, far more than men, take on the role of surrogate parent to their younger siblings. Their roles include cleaning the house, preparing dinner, and helping their siblings with schoolwork. Their work is daily and continuous. The 1.5 generation men seldom participate in motherwork.[1] However, they do participate in monthly rituals such as paying bills and making doctor's appointments.

Although this study addressed gender issues to some degree, the issues associated with sexuality need to be explored further. Based on field studies at Hulas, Punani's, Venice, Angles, and Fusions,[2] there are hundreds of gay, lesbian, and bisexual Korean men and women in Hawai'i. However, due to the "small" community, many remain in the closet. There are several social and cultural obstacles for GLBT Korean Americans. Hawai'i has inherited heterosexist views from the continental United States. At one time, bisexuality and homosexuality in Hawai'i were not seen as deviant or taboo, but rather as integral parts of the fabric of Hawaiian culture. The *'ohana,* or extended family, often included same-sex relationships. The special word for the people in these relationships was *aikane,* but the Hawaiians used other words, such as *ho'okamaka* and *lawakua.*[3] It was not until Western religion was introduced that sexuality became an issue. Although Hawai'i is seen as the same-sex capital, it is still not legal for same-sex couples to marry. Vermont as of this date is the only state that has legalized domestic partner relationships. People in Hawai'i have been waging this struggle for over 10 years.[4]

Although many Hawaiian communities are open to all sexualities, the postcolonization communities continue to hold on to heterosexist views. Thus, GLBTs in Hawai'i have some social spaces where they feel comfortable, but like GLBTs elsewhere, they still do not feel safe expressing their sexuality in the workplace or to their families. Those in the Korean American 1.5 generation have to not only negotiate the generational and ethnic boundaries, but sexual boundaries as well.

One of the challenges that gay 1.5ers face is that the majority of Korean families in Hawai'i are Christian.[5] Growing up in a Christian household, a GLBT 1.5er learns quickly that the family religion does not welcome or accept an alternative sexual identity. In addition, Korean families seldom communicate openly, and do not talk about sex or sexuality with their children. Homosexuality is not foreign to Koreans, or other Asians for that matter;[6] however, the culture is one in which people just do not openly discuss it. In future studies, it would be interesting to study the intersection of sexuality, class, and ethnicity and how the 1.5 generation negotiates the three in Hawai'i.

How Do Children Immigrants Construct a 1.5 Generation Identity?

The resocialization of children into a new culture is common among post-immigrant groups. These youths take part in a series of experiences that move them into adulthood. The process involves the intersection of how 1.5ers view themselves and how others see them. Thus, ethnic identity cannot be based solely on self-identification, but includes acknowledged recognition by other people in the communities. It requires a multidirectional relationship to construct a 1.5 identity. Based on social reinforcement from Koreans and non-Koreans, 1.5ers construct what it means to be Korean American for them and negotiate their ethnic options by switching from Korean to Korean American or local, depending on the situation, parties, and/or place. As the literature suggests, 1.5ers participate in and express a dynamic, fluid ethnic identity that varies with different conditions and situations. For example, to assert a separate identity, 1.5ers speak primarily Korean and Konglish with the first generation and express Korean social cues and behaviors. However, with non-Koreans, 1.5ers express Korean American or local ethnic identity by speaking English or pidgin and interacting in a more egalitarian manner. Yet it is only with other 1.5ers that they are able to construct and express a 1.5 ethnic identity. They speak Konglish, English, and Korean with other 1.5ers and have a shared understanding of what it is like to grow up as and to be a 1.5er.

The family plays a critical role in constructing a 1.5 generation identity. There are various aspects of family life that can have consequential effects on ethnic identity. Whether the parents are married, separated, or widowed; the number of first-, 1.5, or second-generation siblings; the presence of an extended family—these and other factors can influence the family function and dynamics, and 1.5ers' identification with being Korean and Korean American. The family's socioeconomic status also can have direct and indirect influences; thus, for this research the focus was to examine the effects of social class and the family on ethnic identity.

From the family, the child immigrants learn what it means to be Korean. That is, the cultural reinforcement that includes language, values, and sociocultural cues are learned from parents, relatives, and family friends. The children continue to speak Korean, participate with other Koreans, celebrate Korean holidays, and so on. Their expressions of being Korean stem from their family's enforcement of Korean culture. These factors contribute to the identification with being Korean early on in the process of becoming a 1.5er. It is also in the family, however, that the transformation from Korean to Korean American begins. Korean American 1.5ers continue to speak Korean, Konglish, and English; eat and prepare Korean, local, and "American" foods; participate in Korean and American holidays; pursue higher education; and express filial piety in the home. Thus, they construct what it means to be Korean American living with first-generation parents.

The transformation affects working-class and middle-class 1.5ers differently. As working-class 1.5ers become fluent in English, their language ability changes the very nature of the family. Korean American 1.5ers speak Korean with their parents but begin to serve as their translators in order to handle daily household tasks. The parent–child relationship changes as the 1.5ers begin to take care of the household duties, such as paying bills, making appointments, and reading mail. Thus, the working–class parents become more dependent on their children for translation and basic household duties. In addition, with both parents working, the working-class 1.5ers with younger siblings are expected to provide child care for them. While 1.5ers continue to practice traditions of filial piety, their relationship with their parents changes. The 1.5ers become an active voice in the handling of family affairs and manage the household as equals with their parents. They initially take directions from their parents, but later take charge and become the managing force behind the family. Their role shifts from children who are dependent on their parents to an equal voice and member of the family.

The middle-class 1.5ers also begin to transform their Korean ethnic identity to Korean American. However, because these 1.5ers tend to have at least one parent who is fairly fluent in English, they do not only speak Korean to both parents. Instead, they speak Korean to one and Konglish and English to the other, or Konglish and English to both. Consequently, the 1.5er's relationship with parents does not change drastically. The tasks of paying bills and filling out forms are left to the English-fluent parent. However, the 1.5er continues to help the nonfluent parent with translation when the situation warrants. Thus, the parent–child relationship changes more for the working-class families than for the middle class.

The family becomes the setting where Korean American 1.5ers begin to negotiate between their Korean and

Korean American ethnic identities. It is at this part of the process that they begin to learn how to express their bilingual and bicultural abilities in different situations and conditions. It is not until they experience the views of the larger society and their peers that they begin constructing what it means to be Korean American and local.

In school, Korean 1.5ers begin to experience other ethnic and generational groups. They begin to develop close relationships with non-Koreans and locals and to express their American and/or local identity. Some 1.5ers gain an appreciation for the diverse cultures and local lifestyle of Hawai'i, and use pidgin language as a form of expression. Other 1.5ers begin to express their Korean American ethnic identity by speaking standard English, developing relationships with non-Koreans who express more *haole* or "American" attitudes. The 1.5ers' peers offer alternative ethnic options for them to express. They are no longer limited to their expression of being Korean at home; at school, the situation warrants a different ethnic expression.

The school setting also reinforces the 1.5er's shame of coming from an immigrant family. The anti-immigrant sentiment that predominates in society and school sends the message that to fit in one has to be either local or American. Overt discriminatory actions toward FOBs reinforce the shame of being a nonnative. Early memories of being an immigrant combined with their observations of how immigrants continue to be treated by locals push 1.5ers to conform to the "American" or dominant local culture.

Some 1.5ers, who realize that they can pass as local or Asian American, begin to shield their Koreanness by expressing and acting more local or Korean American. They stop associating with other Korean Americans, regardless of generation, and develop close relationships with those who are non-Korean. Their internalization of Korean American stereotypes leads them to distance themselves from Korean communities. It is not until later, when they meet other Koreans who deconstruct their stereotypes, that they begin to appreciate and take pride in being Korean American.

Korean American 1.5ers meet others who can relate to and share their experiences of the process of becoming 1.5. They understand the struggles of living as an immigrant and having first-generation parents. They relate to the stereotypes of the larger society of Asian Americans in general and Koran Americans in particular. The realization that there is a critical mass of 1.5ers who share a common personal history solidifies the feelings of belonging to a group who understand the struggles of constructing a 1.5 ethnic identity.

Through my study, I examined the various processes involved in becoming a 1.5er. Korean immigrant children in Hawai'i are initially first generation. Their status, however, changes in the process of resocializing in a new country, which in turn affects their sense of ethnic identity.

At what point in the process of ethnic identity construction do Korean Americans shift their immigrant first-generation status to 1.5 generation status? This research question addresses the part of the process when 1.5 generation status is actualized. The process of becoming a 1.5er, however, is a long process. Korean Americans do not become or identify as 1.5ers overnight; rather, it is through their interactions with first-generation Koreans, non-Koreans, the larger community, and other 1.5ers that they become conscious of their generational identity. Thus, the transformation is not directly from first to 1.5 generation, but involves a long process, with discovery occurring when 1.5ers gain a sense of collective consciousness. Some children immigrants may never fully develop pride in being 1.5, but remain ashamed and claim a local or American identity. Others may feel that the lack of acceptance from the first or 1.5 generation make them more 1.2 or 1.8 generation. These numbers reflect their feeling that they do not belong with the first or second generation, but fall somewhere in between.

The transformation from immigrant to 1.5er involves various experiences and influences. In the early part of the resocialization process, the family shapes the 1.5ers' identification with being Korean and Korean American. At home, they continue to speak Korean, practice Korean customs, and are exposed to first-generation Korean Americans. Yet it is also in the home that they learn what it means to be Korean American. The changing social environment makes it difficult for the family to maintain the practices of a Korean family; instead, each family member takes on a new role to help transform the family into a Korean American family. Because of the changing relationships between parents and children, the 1.5ers gain an early appreciation for their parents' struggles as immigrants. Their observations of their parents and their newfound responsibilities acquaint 1.5ers with the Korean values of hard work and obligation to family. Korean American 1.5ers often forgo their own childhood interests so that they can care for their siblings and help maintain the family structure. Thus, the transformation from Korean to Korean American identities begins in the family when Korean American 1.5ers encounter conditions requiring them to construct and express an identity that is a hybrid of Korean and Korean American ethnic identities.

As 1.5ers begin to settle and adjust to Hawai'i's culture, their peers and the larger community influence their sense of being Korean American and/or local. As Korean American 1.5ers become more fluent in English and acclimated to Hawai'i's local culture, they learn how non-Koreans and the larger society view immigrants in general and Koreans in particular. The negative stereotypes of Korean Americans influence 1.5ers' disassociative behaviors. At this part of the process, 1.5ers are faced with largely negative images of Korean Americans at a time when they want to belong and "fit in." Thus, they begin to negotiate their ethnic options by expressing Korean or Korean American ethnicity more with their parents, and Korean American,

"American" or *haole*, or local ethnicity more with their peers. Thus, under different conditions, the 1.5ers speak English, pidgin, Korean, or Konglish, depending on the audience and the setting. It is not just their language that 1.5ers switch, but their behaviors as well. With first-generation Korean Americans they are more likely to display honorific behaviors and expressions; with locals they are likely to dress more casually, sit more comfortably, and converse in a more relaxed manner. With "Americanized" or "haolified" Asian Americans and Caucasians, they may attempt to appear more like Asian Americans in the continental United States. The introduction to peers and community is when 1.5ers begin to see that there are other ethnic options for them to navigate.

As 1.5ers enter adulthood, they are introduced to different social settings due to relocation for school or work. They discover other Korean American 1.5ers and feel a sense of solidarity that they had not experienced before and learn to appreciate the uniqueness of their 1.5 ethnic identity. They rethink their previous stereotypes of Korean Americans and replace them with their newfound image of Korean Americans as a heterogeneous group. Furthermore, they individually realize and acknowledge that they are not alone in feeling alienated and marginalized from the first and second generations. There are others like them who share the struggles of becoming a 1.5er. It is at this point that they feel a sense of pride in being Korean American and actualize their 1.5 generational identity as something unique and distinct from first- or second-generation Korean Americans. With other 1.5ers, they can express the various dimensions of who they are interchangeably without explanation or justification. Whereas they show the Korean and Korean American side to their family, and their Korean American and local side to their peers and the larger community, with other Korean American 1.5ers they are able to show all parts of their identity. By freely presenting these various aspects, they express their unique 1.5 ethnic identity, switching from Korean, local, and Korean American without having to explain their reasons for doing so.

It is important to note, however, that not all Korean child immigrants go through the process of becoming a 1.5er. Although the influences of family, the larger society, and peers are a common part of their experience, not all of them meet other 1.5ers in college or professional settings. There are those who are bilingual and bicultural but do not have a positive Korean American ethnic identity. Instead, they remain ashamed of their Korean identity and continue to disassociate from Korean American people and community. Thus, the conditions in which 1.5ers construct a 1.5 ethnic identity have much to do with whom they meet and at what time in their lives they meet them.

Korean American 1.5ers are able to reflect on and re-examine their own stereotypes about Korean Americans when they mature. For example, 1.5ers who are in high school are less likely to rethink their own stereotypes, but instead tend to attempt to conform to the dominant groups. Furthermore, if 1.5ers meet other 1.5ers at one gathering and do not continue their interactions, they are not provided the opportunity to develop close relationships and thus are less likely to become conscious of their 1.5 ethnic identity. Thus, the interaction between 1.5ers must be consistent and nurtured for them to gain a sense of shared personal history. Those who develop close relationships are more likely to become active in their bicultural communities, using their unique 1.5 characteristics to their advantage.

Implications for Future Research

This study has focused on the process by which Korean Americans construct a 1.5 ethnic identity, a process that involves the influences of family, community and peers, and other 1.5 Korean Americans. However, there are other influences that also can be examined, such as church, work, Korean and American media, and identity politics.

Furthermore, this study is based primarily on the 1.5 generation experience in Hawai'i. Future studies may benefit from a comparative study of Korean American 1.5ers in Hawai'i, the West Coast, Midwest, and East Coast. Regional comparisons are likely to illustrate the complexity of ethnic identity. Although this study discussed the various issues facing Korean Americans in New York and California, there are no other empirical studies of the 1.5 generation to compare it with. Further investigation of this generation will help us better understand how the 1.5 generation navigates social and political space in the continental United States. The ethnic options and the methods by which they express different ethnic identities will most likely differ in each region of the United States.

Finally, this study has larger implications for the 1.5 generation group. Although the term *1.5* was originated and initially used by Korean Americans, it is fast becoming vogue in post-1965 immigrant circles. The expression is now used commonly in academic settings to describe the post-1965 immigrant children raised in the United States. What was once a concept used to describe a generational group of Korean Americans has crossed over to other ethnic groups as well. Although this study's focus is on the Korean American 1.5 generation, the process by which they become 1.5ers and the influences in their lives that shape their ethnic identity can be generalized to other ethnic groups as well. That is, the notion of being bilingual and bicultural and the switching of ethnic options do not constitute an exclusively Korean American experience; Filipinos, Latinos, Vietnamese, Cambodians, Haitians, and other immigrant children will experience similar processes of becoming 1.5ers. There are bound to be different factors that help to construct 1.5 ethnic identity, but determining what is most influential in 1.5 ethnic identity construction is what will help us better understand this generation and its community.

The 1.5 generation is an important group to examine in the coming years. With so many children immigrating with their parents, we need to address the needs of the in-between generation. This generation is in a unique position, retaining connections to their homeland and planting roots in a new country. The opportunities for this generation to bridge language barriers and misunderstanding between first-generation communities and the larger society is endless. As a group that has experienced marginalization and alienation while being able to pass as someone on the inside, they are more sensitive to the issues of new immigrants and at the same time to Western values and ideas on how to conduct oneself at work, school, and other mainstream settings. It is when both cultures are embraced and appreciated that 1.5ers gain an idea of what it means to be in between in the United States.

NOTES

Chapter 1: WHO ARE THE 1.5 GENERATION KOREAN AMERICANS?

1. Pronounced "one point five."
2. *Ilchom ose* literally means "one point five" in Korean.
3. Hurh and Kim 1984b.
4. In the January 14, 1999, *Asian Week* cover story, Julie Soo writes, "The term 'juk sing' means 'caught between the notch of a bamboo stick' in Cantonese. It's also how immigrants disparagingly refer to their U.S.-born counterparts: those who genetically share the same ethnicity but are seen as being forever caught in the middle, not fully American because of their looks, but not truly Chinese because of their American attitudes and their lack of proficiency in the Chinese language."
5. Goldsea, "Parsing Asian America," www.goldsea.com/AAD/Parsing/parsing.html.
6. Koh 1994; Hurh 1998; Ryu 1991.
7. Portes and Rumbaut 2001.
8. A combination of Korean and English fused together. Some participate in code switching, switching from one language to another in a given conversation.
9. Hurh 1998.
10. Locals are those who were born and raised in Hawai'i, and have an appreciation and understanding of the island lifestyle and diverse cultures and peoples of Hawai'i.
11. 1991.
12. Lee 1993.
13. Hurh 1998; Kim and Hurh 1993; Koh 1994.

14. Kim and Hurh 1993; Hurh and Kim 1984b; Abelmann and Lie 1995; Min 1996.

15. Hurh and Kim 1984a.

16. Tuan 1999.

17. For a detailed discussion of local identity, read Okamura (1994).

18. This method begins with finding one participant, who refers another participant, and so on. It is the domino effect of finding subjects for a study. Sociologists often use the term *snowball* to create the image of the sample getting bigger and bigger with each referral.

19. The interviews lasted anywhere from 4 to 10 hours, and I met with each interviewee at least three times. The total number of hours spent on informal and formal interviews was close to 200 hours.

20. To ensure confidentiality, the participants' names and some of their personal information have been changed.

21. Due to the nature of my research, I did not carry a tape recorder with me. I initially used a tape recorder but found it distracted the 1.5ers and those around them. Thus, I decided to type out my notes immediately following each observation or interview. Although this approach is not as clearcut as a taped interview, I found that I was able to get rich data as a participant observer; family members and Jaycee members were more "natural" and forthcoming with their thoughts because I did not have the barrier of a tape recorder. Additionally, some respondents did not tell their parents, family, and friends that they were part of my study. Respondents felt that their parents would not be as open to discuss matters if they knew they were under study. The Jaycee respondents felt that a tape recorder would be a distraction in their meetings and functions.

22. Portes 1996; Park 1999.

23. Choy 1979; Patterson 1988.

Chapter 2: KOREAN AMERICANS IN HAWAI'I

1. U.S. Census 2000.

2. Waters 1990.

3. Choy 1979; Patterson 1988.

4. Hurh and Kim 1984a.

5. Abelmann and Lie 1995; Min 1995.

6. Chang 1994; Kim 1994; Abelmann and Lie 1995.

7. Hurh 1998; Min 1995.

8. Choy 1979; Patterson 1988.

9. Results of the 2000 Census are not yet available for Hawai'i.

10. Patterson 1988.

11. Choy 1979.

12. Haas 1998.

13. Patterson 1988.

14. Lee 1993; Patterson 1988; Choy 1979.

15. Patterson 1988; Choy 1979.

16. Patterson 1988.

17. Min 1995.

18. Yu 1983.

19. Yu 1983.

20. Min 1995.

21. 1970, 1980, 1990.

22. Barringer and Cho 1989.

23. Haas 1998.

24. Haas 1998.

25. Okamura 1998a; 1998b.

26. Along with Korean Americans, Samoans, Native Hawaiians, and Filipinos have been left out of the dominant discourse on Asian American issues.

27. Okamura 1998b.

28. Okamura 1998b, p. 16.

29. Yu 1983; Chang 1994.

30. Choy 1979.

31. To better understand the sociopolitical climate in which the Hawaiian land was illegally taken from its peoples, read Haunani-Kay Trask (1999).

32. Tuan 1999.

33. Okamura 1994.

34. http://nani.cis.hawaii.edu/ThemeLocal.HTML

35. Wooden 1981, 1995.

36. Portugese and other western Europeans were also recruited, but in small numbers.

37. Rosa 1996.

38. Oliver Richardson 2000.

39. Listserv discussing what it means to be local.

Chapter 3: SOCIAL CONSTRUCTION OF ETHNIC IDENTITY

1. Glazer and Moynihan 1982; Gordon 1983; Parsons 1964.

2. Hurh 1998.

3. Waters 1990.

4. Mitchell 1974.

5. Nagel 1994; Okamura 1994; Mitchell 1974.

6. Nagel 1994.

7. Nagel 1994; Omi and Winant 1994; Okamura 1981.

8. Lal 1993; Nagel 1994.
9. Lal 1993.
10. Barth 1981; Wallman 1978, 1986.
11. Lal 1993.
12. Fuchs 1990; Patterson 1988.
13. Lal 1993, p. 309.
14. Waters 1990.
15. Atkinson and Sue 1993.
16. Chiu, Feldman, and Rosenthal 1992.
17. Chiu, Feldman, and Rosenthal 1992.
18. Chiu, Feldman, and Rosenthal 1992.
19. Phinney, Chavira, and Williamson 1992.
20. Phinney, Chavira, and Williamson 1992.
21. Phinney, Chavira, and Williamson 1992.
22. Chiu, Feldman, and Rosenthal 1992.
23. Phinny, Chavira, and Williamson 1992; Hurh 1980.
24. Min 1995.
25. Bronfenbrenner 1979, p. 21.
26. Bronfenbrenner 1979, p. 3.
27. Bronfenbrenner 1986.
28. Bronfenbrenner 1979, p. 24.
29. Germain 1994, p. 6.
30. Germain 1994, p. 6.
31. Weinreich 1989.

Chapter 4: KOREAN FAMILIES TRANSFORMED

1. Shon and Ja 1982.
2. Min 1995.
3. Shon and Ja 1982.
4. Kim, Kim, and Hurh 1991.
5. Kim, Kim, and Hurh 1991.
6. Garbarino and Abramowitz 1992.
7. Min 1995.
8. Kim, Kim, and Hurh 1991.
9. Kim and Hurh 1993.
10. Min 1995.
11. Eitzen and Zinn 1989; Kim and Kim n.d.
12. Park, Arnold, Gardner, and Fawcett 1990.
13. Hurh and Kim 1984b; Yu 1983.
14. Min 1995.
15. Steinberg, Dornbush, and Brown 1992.
16. Omi 1993; Abelmann and Lie 1995; Kim 1994.
17. Chang 1994.

18. Abelmann and Lie 1995; Hurh and Kim 1984a.
19. Garbarino and Abramowitz 1992.
20. Chang 1994.
21. Min 1995.
22. Min 1995.
23. Cho and Yada 1994.
24. Min 1995.
25. Yu 1983; Min 1995; Lee 1993.

26. Yu 1983.
27. Min 1995; Yu 1983; Kim and Kim, n.d.
28. Since this statement, David's dad and stepmom have divorced. David says that the reasons have much to do with the fact that his dad marries the "wrong" women for the "wrong" reasons.
29. Min 1995.

Chapter 6: STEREOTYPES AND THEIR IMPACT ON ETHNIC IDENTITY FORMATION

1. The term *haole* was originally used to describe foreigners or outsiders to Hawai'i, but today is synonymous with "white American."
2. Espiritu 1994; Kibria 2002.

Chapter 7: DISCOVERING 1.5 ETHNIC IDENTITY

1. "Buk buk" is the sound that some Koreans make to imitate the accents of Filipinos in Hawai'i. They claim that when Filipinos speak they sound like chickens.
2. http://www.aloha.net/~mt.lai/ajcc/
3. The Honolulu Korean Junior Chamber of Commerce is affiliated with the Hawai'i Jaycees. The Jaycees is not a religious organization and does not discriminate against those who do not believe in God. In addition, the membership is not exclusive to men or persons in business.
4. Many of the individuals who participated in this study are no longer members of the Korean Jaycees. More than half of the members have moved to the continental United States or to Micronesia.
5. An estimate by the current president.
6. Although Sarah was born in Korea, she does not fit the characteristics of a 1.5er since she is not bilingual or bicultural. Sarah jokingly states that she is "1.9" generation.
7. When Jaycees members use the general term *Korean community*, they are referring to the first generation, for until recently there were no other representatives in the community.

8. *Ghe* is an activity that first-generation Korean Americans partake in. This activity, which is considered illegal, involves a group of Korean Americans putting their money into a pool. The members take turns being the keeper of the pool and decide who can borrow from it. There have been instances when people have run off with the pool of money or have failed to pay back the money. *Ghe* is similar to what the Japanese and Filipino communities did during the plantation period.

Chapter 8: WHAT DO THE 1.5 GENERATION KOREAN AMERICANS TELL US?

1. *Motherwork* is a concept that Patricia Hill Collins (2001) came up with to address the multidimensional aspects of being a mother, such as cooking, cleaning, and nurturing children. "Racial ethnic women's motherwork reflects the tensions inherent in trying to foster a meaningful racial identity in children within a society that denigrates people of color" (p. 297).

2. All are gay bars in Honolulu.

3. Morris 1990.

4. *Baehr v. Lewin*, 74 Haw. 645, 852 P.2d 44 (1993), held that a statute denying marriage rights to same-sex couples may violate the state's constitutional equal rights provision (remanded for trial to determine if the state could demonstrate compelling interest to justify the statute). The same case is now styled *Baehr v. Miike*, 80 Haw. 341, 910 P.2d 112 (1996) (denial of intervention applications of clergy and Church of Jesus Christ of Latter-Day Saints); trial was held September 10 through September 26,1996. In November 1998 Hawai'i's constitution was amended to restrict marriage to opposite-sex couples, and in December 1999 the plaintiffs in *Baehr* were accordingly denied relief.

5. There are also a number of Korean Buddhists in Hawai'i, but due to the historical context in which Koreans were brought to the islands, the Methodist church remains the church of choice for Korean immigrants.

6. Korea has no established tradition of overtly discriminatory laws for homsexuals to struggle against. There are no sodomy laws proscribing oral or anal intercourse, largely because these acts have traditionally been considered utterly unmentionable in any public forum or document. The issue of homosexuality has never been brought before Korean courts. No one has mentioned homosexuality in any divorce proceeding, or custody or adoption battle. Nevertheless, conservative pockets exist in Korean society. A popular children's TV show host was dismissed from his job when he became the first celebrity to proclaim his homosexuality to the

public. The number of homosexuals coming out of the closet is growing steadily. Korea witnessed its first lesbian commitment ceremony on November 27, 1995. Nevertheless, homosexuality is still very much underground. "The number of Koreans who come out is very limited. There are probably millions of closet cases. They may go 'cruising' or to bath houses but wouldn't dream to come here. For me personally, only two of my friends know. I haven't told my family, but I think if I did come out my family would eventually come around and accept it. I'm almost 40, so family pressure to get married is nearly behind me. I think they've given up on me" (Travel & Resources: KOREA http://www.utopia-asia.com/tipskor.htm).

203

REFERENCES

Abelmann, Nancy, and John Lie. 1995. *Blue Dreams: Korean Americans and the Los Angeles Riots*. Cambridge MA: Harvard University Press.

Atkinson, D., G. Morten, and D. Sue. 1993. *Counseling American Minorities* (4th ed.). Dubuque, IA: Brown & Benchmark.

Baca Zinn, Maxine. 1990. "Family, Feminism, and Race." *Gender and Society* 4(1): 68–82.

Barringer, Herbert R., and Sung-Nam Cho. 1989. *Koreans in the U.S.: A Fact Book*. Honolulu: Center for Korean Studies, University of Hawai'i.

Barringer, Herbert R., Peter Xenos, and David T. Takeuchi. 1990. "Education, Occupational Prestige, and Income of Asian Americans." *Sociology of Education* 63(1): 27–43.

Barth, F. 1981. "Ethnic Groups and Boundaries." In F. Barth (ed.), *Process and Forms in Social Life: Selected Essays*. London: Routledge & Kegan Paul.

Blumer, H. 1969. *Symbolic Interactionism, Perspective and Method*. Englewood Cliffs, NJ: Prentice-Hall.

Blumer, H., and T. Duster. 1980. "Theories of Race and Social Action." In UNESCO, *Sociological Theories: Race and Colonialism*. Paris: UNESCO.

Bonacich, Edna. 1973. "A Theory of Middleman Minorities." *American Sociological Review* 38(5): 583–594.

Bonacich, Edna, and John Modell. 1980. *The Economic Basis of Ethnic Solidarity*. Berkeley: University of California Press.

Bronfenbrenner, Urie. 1979. *The Ecology of Human Development*. Cambridge, MA: Harvard University Press.

————. 1986. "Ecology of the Family as a Context for Human Development: Research Perspective." *Developmental Psychology* 22(6): 723–742.

Calhoun, C. 1991. "The Problem of Identity in Collective Action." In J. Huber (ed.), *Macro-Micro Linkages in Sociology.* Newbury Park, CA: Sage.

Chan, Sucheng. 1991. *Asian Americans.* Boston: Twayne.

Chang, Edward T. 1994. "America's First Multiethnic 'Riots.'" In K. Aguilar San Juan (ed.), *The State of Asian America: Activism and Resistance in the 1990s.* Boston: South End Press.

Chiu, M., S. S. Feldman, and D. A. Rosenthal. 1992 "The Influence of Immigration on Parental Behavior and Adolescent Distress in Chinese Families Residing in Two Western Nations." *Journal of Research in Adolescence* 2: 205–240.

Cho, Lee-Jay, and Moto Yada. 1994. *Tradition and Change in the Asian Family.* Honolulu: University of Hawai'i Press.

Choy, Bong Youn. 1979. *Koreans in America.* Chicago: Nelson-Hall.

Collins, Patricia Hill. 2001. "Shifting the Center: Race, Class, and Feminist Theorizing about Motherhood." In Susan Ferguson (ed.), *Shifting the Center: Understanding Contemporary Families* (2nd ed.). Mountain View, CA: Mayfield.

Crystal, David. 1989. "Asian Americans and the Myth of the Model Minority." *Social Casework* 70(7): 405–413.

Du Bois, W. E. B. 1961. *The Souls of Black Folk.* Chicago: A.C. McClurg.

Early, G. (ed.). 1993. *Lure and Loathing: Essays on Race Identity and the Ambivalence of Assimilation.* New York: Penguin.

Eitzen, D. Stanley, and Maxine Baca Zinn. 1989. *The Reshaping of America: Social Consequences of the Changing Economy.* Englewood, NJ: Prentice-Hall.

Elder, G. H., Jr. 1984. "Families, Kin and the Life Course: A Sociological Perspective." In R. D. Parke (ed.), *Review of Child Development Research.* Chicago: University of Chicago Press.

Erikson, E. H. 1950. *Childhood and Society.* New York: Norton Press.

Espiritu, Yen Le. 1992. *Asian American Panethnicity.* Philadelphia: Temple University Press.

————. 1994. "The Intersection of Race, Ethnicity, and Class: The Multiple Identities of Second-Generation Filipinos. *Identities: Global Studies in Culture and Power* 1(2–3): 249–273.

Fuchs, L. 1990. *The American Kaleidoscope: Race, Class Ethnicity, and Civic Culture.* Lebanon, NH: University Press of New England.

Gans, H. J. 1979. "Symbolic Ethnicity: The Future of Ethnic Groups and Cultures in America." *Ethnic and Racial Studies* 2: 1–20.

———. 1994. "Symbolic Ethnicity and Symbolic Religiosity: Towards a Comparison of Ethnic and Religious Acculturation." *Ethnic and Racial Studies* 17: 577–592.

Garbarino, James, and Robert H. Abramowitz. 1992. "The Family as a Social System." In James Garbarino (ed.), *Children and Families in the Social Environment*. New York: Aldine de Gruyter.

Gardner, Robert W., Bryant Robey, and Peter C. Smith. 1985. *Asian Americans: Growth, Change and Diversity*. Washington, DC: Population Reference Bureau.

Germain, Carol B. 1994. "Emerging Conceptions of Family Development over the Life Course." *Families in Society: Journal of Contemporary Human Services* 75: 259–267.

Glazer, Nathan. 1976. *The Emergence of American Ethnic Pattern, Affirmative Discrimination: Ethnic Inequality and Public Policy*. New York: Basic Books.

Glazer, Nathan, and Daniel Patrick Moynihan. 1970. *Beyond the Melting Pot: The Negroes, Puerto Ricans, Jews, Italians, and Irish of New York City* (2nd ed.). Cambridge, MA: MIT Press.

Goffman, E. 1968. *Asylums: Essays in the Social Situation of Mental Patients and Other Inmates* (rev. ed.). London: Pelican.

Gordon, Milton. 1964. *Assimilation in American Life*. New York: Oxford University Press.

———. 1983. *America as a Multicultural Society*. Philadelphia: American Academy of Political and Social Science.

Haas, Michael. 1998. *Multicultural Hawai'i: The Fabric of a Multiethnic Society*. New York: Garland.

Hall, William S., and Roy O. Freedle. 1975. *Culture and Language: The Black American Experience*. Washington, DC: Hemisphere.

Hall, W. S., R. Freedle, and W. E. Cross. 1972. *Stages in the Development of a Black Identity* (ACT Research Report No. 50). Iowa City: American Testing Program, Research and Development Division.

Harrison, Algea O., Melvin N. Wilson, Charles J. Pine, Samuel Q. Chan, and Raymond Buriel. 1990. "Family Ecologies of Ethnic Minority Children." *Child Development* 61(2): 347–362.

Hune, Shirley. 1995. "Rethinking Race: Paradigms and Policy Formation." *Amerasia* 21(1–2): 29–40.

Hurh, Won Moo. 1980. "Towards a Korean-American Ethnicity: Some Theoretical Models." *Ethnic and Racial Studies* 3(4): 444–464.

————. 1998. *The Korean Americans*. Westport, CT: Greenwood Press.

Hurh, Won Moo, Hei Chu Kim, and Kwan Chung Kim. 1979. *Assimilation Patterns of Immigrants in the United States: A Case Study of Korean Immigrants in the Chicago Area.* Washington, DC: University Press of America.

Hurh, Won Moo, and Kwang Chung Kim. 1984a. "Adhesive Sociocultural Adaptation of Korean Immigrants in the U.S.: An Alternative Strategy of Minority Adaptation." *International Migration Review* 18: 188–216.

————. 1984b. *Korean Immigrants in America: A Structural Analysis of Ethnic Confinement and Adhesive Adaptation.* Rutherford, NJ: Fairleigh Dickinson University.

Hutnik, N. 1991. *Ethnic Minority Identity: A Social Psychological Perspective.* Oxford: Oxford University Press.

Kibria, Nazli. 2002. *Becoming Asian American.* Baltimore: John Hopkins University Press.

Kim, Elaine. 1994. "Home Is Where the Han Is: A Korean American Perspective on the Los Angeles Upheavals." *Social Justice* 20: 1–21.

Kim, Kwang Chung, and Won Moo Hurh. 1983. "Korean Americans and the 'Success' Image: A Critique." *Amerasia* 10(2): 3–21.

————. 1993. "Beyond Assimilation and Pluralism: Syncretic Sociocultural Adaptation of Korean Immigrants in the U.S." *Ethnic and Racial Studies* 16(4): 696–712.

Kim, Kwang Chung, and Shin Kim. N.d. *Emergence of the Extended Conjugal Family: An Analysis of Korean Immigrants' Family/Kinship System.* Unpublished manuscript.

Kim, Kwang Chung, Shin Kim, and Won Moo Hurh. 1991. "Filial Piety and Intergeneration Relationship in Korean Immigrant Families." *International Journal of Aging and Human Development* 33(3): 233–245.

Kitano, Harry H. L., and A. Kikumura. 1980. "The Japanese American Family." In R. Endo, Stanley Sue, and N. Wagner (eds.), *Asian Americans: Social and Psychological Perspectives.* Palo Alto, CA: Science and Behavior Books.

Kitano, Harry, and Stanley Sue. 1973. "The Model Minorities." *Journal of Social Issues* 29(2): 1–10.

Kitano, H. H., W. T. Yeung, L. Chai, and H. Hatanaka. 1984. "Asian American Interracial Marriage." *Journal of Marriage and the Family* 46(1): 179–190.

Koh, Tong-He. 1994. "Ethnic Identity in First, 1.5, and Second Generation Korean-Americans." In *Korean Americans: Conflict and Harmony.* Chicago: North Park College and Theological Seminary.

208

Lal, B. B. 1983. "Perspectives on Ethnicity: Old Wine in New Bottles." *Ethnic and Racial Studies* 6(2): 185–198.

———. 1990. *The Romance of Culture in an Urban Civilization: Robert E. Park on Race and Ethnic Relations in Cities.* New York: Routledge.

———. 1993. "The Celebration of Ethnicity as a Critique of American Life: Opposition to Robert E. Park's View of Cultural Pluralism and Democracy." In R. Gubert and L. Tomasi (eds.), *Robert E. Park and the "Melting Pot."* Trento, Italy: Reverdito Edizioni.

Lee, Yoon Mo. 1993. "Interorganizational Context of the Korean Community for the Participation of the Emerging Generation." In *The Emerging Generation of Korean-American.* Seoul: Kyung Hee University Press.

Lowe, Lisa. 1991. "Heterogeneity, Hybridity, Multiplicity: Marking Asian American Differences." *Diaspora: A Journal of Transitional Studies* 1(1): 24–44.

Marable, Manning. 1993. "Beyond Racial Identity Politics: Towards a Liberation Theory for Multicultural Democracy." *Race and Class* 35: 112–130.

Min, Pyong Gap. 1994. "Major Issues Relating to Asian American Experience." In *Asian Americans.* Boston: Twayne.

———. 1995. *Asian Americans: Contemporary Trends and Issues.* Thousand Oaks, CA: Sage.

———. 1996. *Caught in the Middle.* Berkeley: University of California Press.

Mitchell, J. C. 1974. "Perception of Ethnicity and Ethnic Behavior: An Empirical Exploration." In Abner Cohen (ed.), *Urban Ethnicity.* London: Tavistock.

Modood, Tariq. 1994. *Changing Ethnic.* London: Policy Studies Institute.

Morris, Robert J. "Aikane: Accounts of Hawaiian Same-Sex Relationships in the Journals of Captain Cook's Third Voyage (1776–80)." *Journal of Homosexuality* 19(4): 21–54.

Nagel, Joane. 1994. "Constructing Ethnicity: Creating and Recreating Ethnic Identity and Culture." *Social Problems* 41(1): 152–176.

Okamura, Jonathan. 1981. "Situational Ethnicity." *Ethnic and Racial Studies* 4(4): 452–465.

———. 1994. "Why There Are No Asian Americans in Hawai'i: The Continuing Significance of Local Identity." *Social Process in Hawai'i* 35: 161–178.

———. 1998a. "Beyond Adaptationism: Immigrant Filipino Ethnicity in Hawai'i." In Franklin Ng (ed.), *Adaptation, Acculturation, and Transnational Ties among Asian Americans.* New York: Garland.

209

———. 1998b. "Social Stratification." In Michael Haas (ed.), *Multicultural Hawai'i: The Fabric of a Multiethnic Society.* New York: Garland.

Oliver Richardson, Yumiko. 2000. "Construction, Representation and the Politics of Being 'Local' in Hawai'i." Paper presented at the 25th Annual Conference of the Association of Social Anthropologists of Aotearoa/New Zealand.

Olzak, Susan. 1985. "Ethnicity and Ethnic Collective Behavior." In Louis Kriesberg (ed.), *Research in Social Movements, Conflict, and Change.* Greenwich, CT: JAI Press.

Omatsu, Glenn. 1994. "The 'Four Prisons' and the Movements of Liberation: Asian American Activism from the 1960's to the 1990's." In Karin Aguilar San Juan (ed.), *The State of Asian America: Activism and Resistance in the 1990's.* Boston: South End Press.

Omi, Michael. 1993. "Out of the Melting Pot and Into the Fire: Race Relations Policy." In *The State of Asian Pacific America: Policy Issues to the Year 2020.* Los Angeles: LEAP Asian Pacific American Public Policy Institute.

Omi, Michael, and Howard Winant. 1994. *Racial Formation in the United States from the 1960's to the 1990's.* New York: Free Press.

Park, Kyeyoung. 1999. "'I Really Do Feel I'm 1.5!' The Construction of Self and Community by Young Korean Americans." *Amerasia* 25(1): 139–164.

Park, Insook, Fred Arnold, Robert Gardner, and James Fawcett. 1990. *Korean Immigrants and U.S. Immigration Policy: A Predeparture Perspective.* Honolulu: East West Center.

Park, Robert. 1950. Race and Culture. Glencoe, IL: Free Press.

Parsons, Talcott, 1964. *Social Structure and Personality.* New York: Free Press of Glencoe.

Patterson, Wayne. 1988. *The Korean Frontier in America: Immigration to Hawai'i, 1896–1910.* Honolulu: University of Hawai'i Press.

Phinney, Jean. 1990. "Ethnic Identity in Adolescents and Adults: Review of Research." *Psychological Bulletin* 108(3): 499–514.

Phinney, Jean S., Victoria Chavira, and Lisa Williamson. 1992. "Acculturation Attitudes and Self-Esteem among High School and College Students." *Youth & Society* 23(3): 299–312.

Portes, Alejandro. 1996. *The New Second Generation.* New York: Russell Sage Foundation.

Portes, Alejandro, and Rumbaut, Rubén G. 1990. *Immigrant America: A Portrait.* Berkeley: University of California Press.

———. 2001. *Legacies: The Story of Immigrant Second Generation.* Berkeley: University of California Press and New York: Russell Sage Foundation.

Rosa, John Chock. 1996. "'Local' in the Thirties: The Massie Case and Hawai'i's Asian Pacific Americans." Paper presented at the Association for Asian American Studies Joint Regional Conference, Honolulu, March 24–26.

Rue, David S. 1993. "Depression and Suicidal Behavior among Asian Whiz Kids." In *The Emerging Generation of Korean-American.* Seoul: Kyung Hee University Press.

Ryu, Charles. 1991. "1.5 Generation." In Joan F. J. Lee (ed.), *Asian American Experiences in the United States.* Jefferson, NC: McFarland, pp. 50–54.

San Juan, Karin Aguilar (ed.). 1994. *The State of Asian America: Activism and Resistance in the 1990's.* Boston: South End Press.

Shon, Steven, and Davis Ja. 1982. "Asian Families." In Monica McGoldrick (ed.), *Ethnicity and Family Therapy.* New York: Guilford Press.

Smith, Michael Peter, and Joe R. Feagin. 1995. *The Bubbling Cauldron.* Minneapolis: University of Minnesota Press.

Sowell, Thomas. 1994. *Race and Culture.* New York: Basic Books.

Spickard, Paul R., and Rowena Fong. 1995. "Pacific Islander Americans and Multiethnicity: A Vision of America's Future?" *Social Forces* 73(4): 1365–1383.

Steinberg, L., S. Dornbush, and B. Brown. 1992. "Ethnic Differences in Adolescent Achievement: An Ecological Perspective." *American Psychologist* 47(6): 723–729.

Takagi, Dana Y. 1990. "From Discrimination to Affirmative Action: Facts in the Asian American Admissions Controversy." *Social Problems* 37(4): 578–592.

———. 1992. *Retreat from Race: Asian-Americans and Racial Politics.* New Brunswick, NJ: Rutgers University Press.

Tamura, Eileen H. 1994. *Americanization, Acculturation, and Ethnic Identity.* Champaign: University of Illinois Press.

Taylor, Ronald L. 1994. *Minority Families in the U.S.* Englewood Cliffs, NJ: Prentice Hall.

Tizard, B., and A. Phoenix. 1993. *Black, White or Mixed Race?* New York: Routledge.

Tonkin, E., M. McDonald, and M. Chapman. 1989. *History and Ethnicity* (ASA monograph). London: Routledge.

Trask, Haunani-Kay. 1999. *From a Native Daughter: Colonialism and Sovereignty in Hawai'i.* Honolulu: University of Hawai'i Press.

Tuan, Mia. 1999. *Forever Foreigners or Honorary Whites?* New Brunswick, NJ: Rutgers University Press.

Turner, R., and L. Killian. 1972. *Collective Behavior.* Englewood Cliffs, NJ: Prentice-Hall.

Umemoto, Karen. 1989. "'On Strike' San Francisco State College Strike, 1968–1969: The Role of Asian American Students." *Amerasia* 15: 3–41.

U.S. Census. 1970, 1980, 1990.

U.S. Commission on Civil Rights. 1988. *Economic Status of Americans of Asian Descent: An Exploratory Investment.* Washington, DC: Government Printing Office.

Verkuyten, Maykel. 1995. "Self-Esteem, Self-Concept Stability, and Aspects of Ethnic Identity among Minority and Majority Youth in the Netherlands." *Journal of Youth and Adolescence* 24(2): 155–175.

Verkuyten, M., and G. A. Kwa. 1994. "Ethnic Self-identification and Psychological Well-Being Among Minority Youth in the Netherlands." *International Journal of Adolescence and Youth* 5: 19–34.

Volkardt, E. H. (ed.). 1951. *Social Behavior and Personality: Contributions of W. I. Thomas to Theory and Social Research.* New York: Social Science Research Council.

Wallman, S. 1978. "The Boundaries of 'Race': Processes of Ethnicity in England." *Man* 13(2): 200–217.

———. 1986. "Ethnicity and the Boundary Process in Context." In J. Rex and D. Mason (eds.), *Theories of Race and Ethnic Relations.* Cambridge: Cambridge University Press.

Waters, M. C. 1990. *Ethnic Options.* Los Angeles: University of California Press.

Weinreich, P. 1989. *A Case Study Approach to the Analysis of Identity Structure.* Bristol, England: University of Bristol, SSRC, Research Unit on Ethnic Relations.

Whyte, William Foote. 1984. *Learning from the Field.* Beverly Hills, CA: Sage.

Williams, Raymond. 1976. *Keywords: A Vocabulary of Culture and Society* (rev. ed.). New York: Oxford University Press.

Wirth, L. 1964. "Louis Wirth on Cities and Social Life: Selected Papers." Chicago: University of Chicago Press.

Wong, Morrison. 1986. "Post 1965 Asian Immigration: Where Do They Come from, Where Are They Now and Where Are They Going?" *Annals of the American Academy of Political and Social Sciences* 487.

Wooden, Wayne S. 1981. *What Price Paradise? Changing Social Patterns in Hawai'i.* Washington, DC: University Press of America.

———. 1995. *Return to Paradise: Continuity and Change in Hawai'i.* Washington, DC: University Press of America.

Yamanaka, Keiko, and Kent McClelland. 1994. "Earning the Model-Minority Image: Diverse Strategies of Economic

Adaptation by Asian American Women." *Ethnic and Racial Studies* 17(1): 79–114.

Yong-Jin, Won. 1994. "Model Minority Strategy and Asian-Americans' Tactics." *Korea Journal* 57.

Yu, Eui-Young. 1983. "Korean Communities in America: Past, Present, and Future." *Amerasia* 10(2): 23–52.

Zastrow, Charles, and Karen Larst-Ashman. 1990. *Understanding Human Behavior and the Social Environment.* Chicago: Nelson-Hall.

Zhou, Min, and Carl L. Bankston. 1998. *Growing Up American.* New York: Russell Sage Foundation.

213

INDEX

Kim, Kwang Chung, 1, 62–63, 71, 78
Kim, Shin, 62–63
King, Rodney, 79
Kitano, Harry, 83, 85–86
"knee-high generation," 1, 83–84. *See also* 1.5 generation
"Konglish," 4, 9, 22, 104, 119; defined, 197. *See also* code switching
Korea: economic boom of 1980s, 40; economic crash of 1998, 40, 130; economy, 30, 129–130
"Koreamoku." *See* Keʻeaumoku Street
Korean (identity): ethnic hierarchy, position in, 31; maintaining, role of family in, 12, 93–94
Korean (language): conversational, 8; literacy, 8. *See also* bilingualism; language
Korean American (identity): 13–14, 131–134, 149; family role in formation of, 12, 108; filial practices and individual goals, 124; images of, 134, 164; transformation to, 116–121, 187–189
"Korean bar." *See* hostess bar
Korean Chamber of Commerce, 136
Korean Directory of Hawaiʻi, 36–39
Korean Junior Chamber of Commerce. *See* Jaycees, Korean
Koreanness: basis of, 72; dress, 161; expression, 75, 190; language, 161; occupation, 161; privileging, 13; social network, 161
Kwa, G. A., 54

language: accent, 5; acquisition, 103–104; barrier, 74, 147, 161, 168–169, 178; culture and, 2; English, 102; Konglish, 4, Korean, 8, 102, 169; as obstacle, 102–103; pidgin, 44, 144. *See also* code switching
larger society. *See* dominant society
Locals (in Hawaiʻi), 43–46, 142–145, 149, 184, 197n. 1:10
Los Angeles riots, 1992, 79

marginalization of 1.5ers, 4, 14, 156, 172, 180, 182
marriage: financial role of women and, 87; preferences of 1.5ers, 84–86; same-sex, 186
Massie Trial, 44
"melting pot." *See* assimilation
Methodist Church, 29. *See also* Christians
methodology, 20
middle-class family, 185, 187; case studies, 109–123; defined, 92–93
Min, Pyong Gap, 86–87
minority identity development model, 55
Mitchell, J. C., 50
Morten, G., 56–57
multiculturalism, 184

Native Hawaiian, 31
Negro-to-black conversion experience, 55
neighborhood, images of Koreans, 98, 113–116
newspaper, Korean, 136

O'ahu, 135
occupation, 39–40; advantages
of ethnicity; 157; cate-
gories, 32; choice of, 42;
family, effect on, 80; language, effect on, 103; of
men, 32; professional, 30,
32; table, 35; of women, 32
Okamura, Jonathan, 16, 31, 43
one-point-five generation. *See*
1.5 generation
optional situation theory,
48–49, 52–53
"outside/inside" status, 143,
147

pan-Asians. *See* Asian
Americans
"paper" Chinese, 29
parent-child relationship,
105–109, 189; and
parental dedication, 123;
and parental dependence,
106, in middle class,
121–125
participant observation, 17
participants, 19–20
passing, 5, 11, 14, 152
peers, 139–147, 190; choice
of, 141–142
philanthropy, 177
Phinney, Jean, 54, 59
pidgin. *See* language, pidgin
plantation: labor disputes, 29;
life on, 44; legacy,
184–185
prejudice, internalized,
155–156
pride, 185
privilege, of minority groups,
31
processual experience, 68. *See*
also 1.5 generation identity
formation.
public housing, 98

race relations: in continental
United States, 43; in
Hawai'i, 43
racism, 10; internalized, 48
research goals, 183
resentment between
generations, 180
resocialization, 5, 12, 15, 60,
187–190
Richardson, Yumiko Oliver,
45
ridicule, 97, 141
Rosa, John, 44

same-sex marriage, 186,
202n. 8:4
same-sex relationships, 88
Samoans, 31
sample, 19–20. *See also*
snowball sampling
Sansei, 45
school: private, 140, professional, 140, public, 99,
140; vocational, 140. *See*
also education
second generation: characteristics of, 11; defined, 2;
relationship with first
generation, 178–179;
social network, 136
segregation: ethnic, 61, 101;
and native English
speakers, 145
sex work, 130, 132
shame, 102, 128, 141, 145,
147–149, 156, 173,
175–176; and adolescence,
57
snowball sampling, 18, 198n.
1:18
social class, 184, 188. *See also*
middle-class family;
working-class family
social construction theory,
50–51

221

ABOUT THE AUTHOR

Mary Yu Danico received her doctorate in sociology from the University of Hawai'i at Mānoa. She is currently associate professor of sociology in the psychology and sociology department at California State Polytechnic University, Pomona. She has also co-written *Asian American Issues* as part of the Contemporary U.S. Ethnic Issues Series with Greenwood Press. Her current research project examines low-income Asian American communities, youths, and organizations in Orange County.